Contents

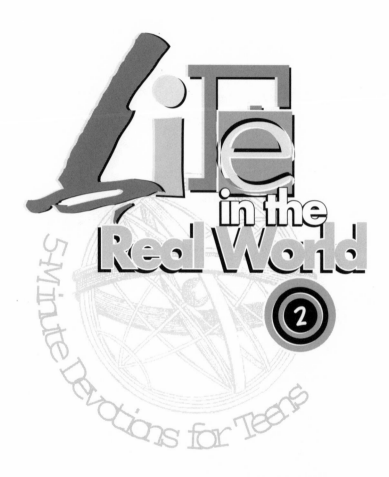

Life in the Real World

in the
Real World

2

5-Minute Devotions for Teens

Eileen Ritter

CONCORDIA PUBLISHING HOUSE • SAINT LOUIS

Copyright © 1999 Concordia Publishing House
3558 S. Jefferson Avenue, St. Louis, MO 63118-3968
Manufactured in the United States of America

Library of Congress Cataloging-in-Publication Data

Ritter, Eileen, 1943-
    Life in the real world 2 : 5-minute devotions for teens / Eileen Ritter.
        p. cm.
    SUMMARY: A collection of meditations with scripture references, practical applications, and prayers, focusing on such real-life issues as friends and family, forgiveness, pollution, creation, and peer pressure.
    ISBN 0-570-05348-x
    1. Teenagers—Prayer-books and devotions—English. [1. Prayer books and devotions.] I. Title.
    BV4850 .R575 1999
    242'.63—dc21   98-41223
                                                                            AC

4   5   6   7   8   9   09   08   07   06   05   04

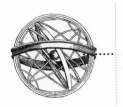

Now Jesus Himself was about thirty years old when He began His ministry. *Luke 3:23*

Something to Think About

Hey, Lord—remember me? Down here, trying my best to live as You would want, trying my best to make it through the week. But things aren't going so well, and I could really use Your help. I mean, *really*.

Lord? Can You hear me? Will You help me? I know You've promised to help, but some-times—well, a lot of times lately, it seems like You've made other plans. When is it my turn for Your attention?

Lord? Lord, please, ... anytime now. I really need You!

Into the Word

Our idea of perfect timing usually doesn't seem to be God's, does it? For another example of this conflict between our timing and God's timing, remember Mary. God's angel, Gabriel, had appeared to her in Nazareth one day when she was very young, perhaps no more than 14 years old. The angel's news changed her life forever—she would have a baby boy, and He would be God's own Son. What a privilege and joy to be the mother of the Messiah!

There was the unexpected trip to Bethlehem, the visitation of the shepherds, and the adoration of the kings. Old Simeon had recognized the Baby for who He really was, and Anna too when they took little Jesus to the temple. But aside from these instances, nothing revealed Mary's child as the Son of God. Jesus grew up just like all the other boys in Nazareth. Mary probably wondered: When would God reveal her Son's identity to everyone? When would He begin His work of salvation?

In My Life

You believe the promises God has made to you: to be with you in times of trouble, to make everything work together for good, to answer your prayers, to make you triumph over your enemies. But don't you get a little impatient?

Wait, as Mary did. In God's time, Jesus began His ministry, taught, healed, suffered, died, and rose again. In God's time, He will keep all His promises to you.

Prayer

My times are in Your hands, Lord. Please give me patience to trust in the wisdom of Your timing. In Jesus' name. Amen.

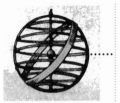

Near the cross of Jesus stood His mother, His mother's sister, Mary the wife of Clopas, and Mary Magdalene. When Jesus saw His mother there, and the disciple whom He loved standing nearby, He said to His mother, "Dear woman, here is your son," and to the disciple, "Here is your mother." From that time on, this disciple took her into his home.
John 19:25–27

Something to Think About

"Wow! Can you believe we're seniors?" Julie asked, coming up to Kristi the first day of school.

"Not at all. It's kind of scary, don't you think? Now we have to start figuring out what to do after graduation. You know, college and everything."

Julie shrugged. "I already know what I'm doing, getting out of this town and never coming back."

"Are you serious? How are you going to do it on your own?"

"It doesn't matter. I just know that some-way, somehow I'll be incredibly rich and success-ful. I'll marry some gorgeous guy, and I'll live hap-pily ever after."

Kristi laughed. "Yeah, that'll happen. But seriously, you'd never come back here? What about your family?"

"Why do they matter? I'll be able to take care of myself. They'll be able to take care of them-selves. Life will be perfect."

In My Life

Sometimes, in our pursuit of success, it becomes easy to forget about all the people who helped us on our way. Friends, teachers, and family fall by the wayside as we focus only on our goals—and only on ourselves

But that's OK, right? Those others, especially our parents who have always been able to take care of themselves, they'll be fine, right?

Well, by human standards, Jesus was not as successful as some us dream of being. But by divine reckoning, He did what no one else could do. He had, by His death, taken the punishment for the sins of all people who had ever lived and ever would live. Yet even as He was dying, He provided for His mother by lovingly placing her into the hands of His friend, John.

It's strange to think we would have to care for our parents in the same way they have always cared for us. But no one can ever live alone, and we can never achieve the success we dream of alone. We need the grace and love of Christ, and we need the love and support of our friends and family. But they will always need our love and support too.

Prayer Thought

As you remember times when you have not shown your love for your parents, ask for God's forgiveness. Then seek His help in finding ways to care for your family.

In the beginning God created the heavens and the earth ... God saw all that He had made, and it was very good. *Genesis 1:1,31*

Something to Think About

Imagine the most exotic travel posters you've ever seen. Then throw in the peace and harmony of a *National Geographic* animal special. The world God created surpasses anything we have seen or can imagine. Even God, the ultimate perfectionist, pronounced it very good.

But look around at God's perfect creation today. Flowing rivers are often too polluted by sewage to support human or animal life. The Cuyahoga River near Cleveland once caught fire because of industrial pollution. Sometimes entire mountain ranges seem to disappear because of the smog. The air in Los Angeles is often so polluted that it hides the San Gabriel mountains only a few miles away. The creatures God created, both animal and human, prey upon each other and struggle for survival. Extinction becomes a real possibility for many forms of life, including us.

Is there a contradiction here? God's "very good" world doesn't look so wonderful anymore. What happened?

It would be easy to blame corporations or governments, and they do share the guilt. But doesn't it start with our carelessly tossed soda cans and gum wrappers? Selfishness, greed, laziness, self-indulgence—God calls these basic attributes of human nature sin. Ever since sin entered the garden God created and the hearts of His creatures, we have grabbed what we can for ourselves and struck out violently against each other. We're all guilty.

Into the Word

But God had a plan for the world He made and loved. Jesus explained it to Nicodemus: "For God so loved the world that He gave His one and only Son, that whoever believes in Him shall not perish but have eternal life" (John 3:16).

Because Jesus lived, died, and rose again, peace and harmony have been reestablished between us and God. Rivers still burn. Garbage piles up in landfills. People and animals die. The final victory, however, has been won. Jesus said, "You are already clean because of the word I have spoken to you" (John 15:3). Because of His cleansing and saving grace, we can look forward to a new heaven and a new earth—the home of the righteous. (See 2 Peter 3:13.) And that is very good.

Prayer

Forgive me, Lord, for my selfishness and greed, my carelessness for Your creation, and my lack of love for Your creatures. Create in me a pure and clean heart, and help me to look forward to the new heaven and earth, where I will be with You forever in righteousness. For Jesus' sake. Amen.

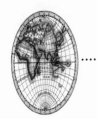

I delight greatly in the LORD; my soul rejoices in my God. For He has clothed me with garments of salvation and arrayed me in a robe of righteousness. *Isaiah 61:10*

Something to Think About

Clothes! Owning and wearing the right ones can make the difference between being part of the "in" crowd and being hopelessly left out. And certain articles of clothing can definitely affect your mood—a hat you wear when you're feeling carefree and goofy, or an old flannel shirt you put on for comfort when you're feeling down.

Clothes! On the list of all-time battle starters with parents, they rank right up there with hairstyles and music preferences. "Do you always have to look so sloppy?" "You paid how much for that shirt?" "You can't wear that. It's too short!" "Too long!" "Too tight!" "Too loose!"

An old proverb tells us that "Clothes make the man." While we know that what's inside the clothes—the person—is what really counts, we have to admit clothes do make a difference in how we treat people—and how they treat us. People seem to respect us more when we dress nicely. We may even feel better about ourselves when we like what we're wearing.

Into the Word

In Matthew 22, Jesus tells a parable about a king who prepared a wedding banquet for his son. The invited guests declined his invitation, so he sent his servants out to invite everyone they found on the street corners. Finally his hall was filled with guests.

When the king entered the noisy banquet hall, he noticed one guest not wearing wedding clothes. The king asked why he wasn't dressed properly, but the guest had no response to the king's question. So the angry king demanded that he be bound, hand and foot, and thrown out into the darkness.

Seems harsh, doesn't it? Perhaps, except the king himself had provided the guest's clothes. By refusing to wear them, the guest rejected the king's gift.

The most important clothes we can ever wear or "own" are those given to us by *our* King. "For all of you who were baptized into Christ have clothed yourselves with Christ" (Galatians 3:27); in other words, through His death and resurrection, we are covered with the perfect righteousness of Christ.

And dressed in *this* righteousness, in *these* clothes, how can we help but feel better about ourselves?

Prayer

Jesus, thank You for giving me the best clothes I could ever hope to own—Your righteousness. Help me to live accordingly, to Your glory. Amen.

On Herod's birthday the daughter of Herodias danced for them and pleased Herod so much that he promised with an oath to give her whatever she asked. Prompted by her mother, she said, "Give me here on a platter the head of John the Baptist." The king was distressed, but because of his oaths and his dinner guests, he ordered that her request be granted and had John beheaded in the prison. His head was brought in on a platter and given to the girl, who carried it to her mother. *Matthew 14:6-11*

Into the Word

Herod had really backed himself into a corner this time. John the Baptist, that crazy prophet who had drawn such crowds with his preaching by the Jordan River, had pushed too many buttons too close to Herod's private life. When John attacked his marriage to his brother's ex-wife, Herodias, Herod gave in to his wife's fury and arrested John. But pressure from John's many Jewish followers made Herod afraid to execute him.

Now at the celebration for Herod's birthday, Herodias' daughter performed a crowd-pleasing dance. In front of all of his friends, Herod promised to give the girl anything she desired. Prompted by her mother, she demanded John's head on a platter.

Tension filled the room. The birthday guests waited eagerly to see what Herod would do; mother and daughter could almost taste their victory; and Herod sat amid them all, sweating profusely. He wanted to spare John's life, but was not willing to appear the fool in front of his friends. What to do?

Something to Think About

Karen could feel her heart start to race. She knew she never should have gotten herself into this situation, but it was too late to go back now.

Jason had set down five shots of Tequila for each of them on the table and the entire room was chanting her name. There was no way to back out of her dare to outdrink Jason, but she knew there was no way her body could handle that much alcohol.

"Ready?" Jason asked. "Or are you going to chicken out like last time?"

She really did not want to do this ...

In My Life

Think about how often you've heard that you should not cave in to peer pressure, and then think about how many times you have.

You're not alone. The need to fit in, to rise to the challenge of others, exists in all of us. And as much as we may try to rise above the pressure, we still find ourselves in bad situations, caving in over and over again.

We cave in because we're sinful human beings who need our Savior's help. Thankfully, we can have faith that when we confess our sins to Christ, He forgives us. Furthermore, we know He will be there to help us resist the temptation next time we find ourselves in a pressure-filled situation.

Prayer

Lord Jesus, forgive me for caving in to pressure from my peers. Give me the wisdom to avoid situations in which I might sin because of peer pressure and the courage to do what is right even in the face of ridicule or embarrassment. Amen.

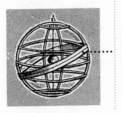

O LORD my God, I take refuge in You; save and deliver me from all who pursue me, or they will tear me like a lion and rip me to pieces with no one to rescue me. *Psalm 7:1-2*

Into the Word

David knew all about enemies. As a shepherd boy, he had fought lions and bears who tried to steal lambs from his father's flock. With God's help, he defeated Goliath with a slingshot and five smooth stones. For years he skirmished with Saul's army, with the Philistines, and Israel's other unfriendly neighbors. Later in his life, he even had to defend himself against his own son, Absalom, who tried to usurp his throne.

David's words in Psalm 7 reflect his quiet trust in God's power to protect him from his enemies. David knew that he would not be disgraced or defeated because he never faced his enemies alone.

Something to Think About

Usually when we think about enemies, instead of Philistine giants or unfriendly armies, we think about the rival football team across town, or the friend who turned out not to be a friend and started spreading rumors about us, or the class bully who has never left us alone. These people do make our lives more difficult—and can cause us a great deal of heartache and pain.

But spiritually speaking, we have an even greater problem on our hands. Peter warns us, "Be self-controlled and alert. Your enemy the devil prowls around like a roaring lion looking for someone to devour" (1 Peter 5:8). His favorite snack? The children of God.

Our arch enemy's prime objective is to oppose God and His way of living, especially in our lives. And Satan has an arsenal of tools at his disposal: temptations like popularity, lust, material possessions; people in our lives who aren't concerned with living God-pleasing lives; even ourselves—our desires, our self-esteem (or lack of it), our weak and sinful nature. This arch enemy has tempted everyone who has ever tried to follow God, including Jesus Himself. And everyone, except Jesus, has lost skirmishes to him. Sounds hopeless, doesn't it?

Peter says it isn't. "Resist [Satan], standing firm in the faith ... And the God of all grace, who called you to His eternal glory in Christ, after you have suffered a little while, will Himself restore you and make you strong, firm and steadfast" (1 Peter 5:9–10).

And we have all the hope in the world, because even as we trust God will be with us as we battle our enemies, we know the final outcome has already been decided through Jesus' death and resurrection.

Prayer

To You, O Lord, I pray. Don't let my enemies succeed; don't give them victory over me. Forgive me for the times I have tried to face temptation without You and have failed. Be with me when I am tempted, and make me strong enough to resist temptation. For You have defeated sin, death, and the devil himself for me. Amen.

"Why do you look at the speck of sawdust in your brother's eye and pay no attention to the plank in your own eye? How can you say to your brother, 'Brother, let me take the speck out of your eye,' when you yourself fail to see the plank in your own eye? You hypocrite, first take the plank out of your eye, and then you will see clearly to remove the speck from your brother's eye." Luke 6:41–42

Something to Think About

"This is the last time I'm telling you," Tim yelled at his little brother. "I don't want you coming in my room and taking my things. You took my CD player and CDs without even asking. Last week you borrowed my basketball and didn't bring it back. Use your own stuff and leave mine alone."

Tim dropped his dad's new wrench set on the dresser and plopped down on his bed. *Maybe a big lock would keep Mike out of my room*, he thought. *I'll complain to Mom again, and she'll get after him.* Tim reached for his pillow, but his hand found one of the car magazines his Dad had told him to leave in the family room.

Into the Word

Jesus used sawdust specks and wooden planks to teach a lesson about criticizing. He knew that we often criticize others to call attention away from the wrong we have done. Our sins don't seem so terrible when we point out the sins of others.

Jesus didn't want His followers to ignore wrongdoing. In Matthew 18:15–17, He gave step-by-step directions for confronting a fellow Christian who has sinned in order to bring him or her to repentance and forgiveness. This kind of Christian confrontation focuses on Christ and His forgiveness. In contrast, pointing fingers—concentrating on someone else's sin—keeps us from confessing our own and receiving God's forgiveness.

In My Life

What kinds of "specks" are the easiest for you to find and point out in other people's lives? How might each of these specks be related to "planks" in our own lives?

When specks and planks give you "eye" trouble, remember to "focus" on Jesus, who carried all our specks and planks to the wooden cross of Calvary.

Prayer

Heavenly Father, I confess to You all I have done wrong. Forgive me for the sake of Your Son, Jesus, who died for me. Help me not to confront others merely to point out their sins, but rather to bring them to forgiveness through Your Son. This I pray in Jesus' name. Amen.

For I, the LORD your God, am a jealous God, punishing the children for the sin of the fathers to the third and fourth generation of those who hate me. *Exodus 20:5b*

Something to Think About

Kelly knew Brad was coming up behind her, but she tried to ignore him.

"Hey, Kel," he said, hugging her from behind. "How was practice?"

Kelly tried to shrug him off. "Fine."

Brad moved quickly away. "All righty, then, what's wrong?"

Kelly hesitated. His voice sounded like he didn't have a clue, but one could never really tell with Brad. "I saw you talking to Kim earlier."

"Yeah, so?"

He really didn't seem to get it. "Did you have to get so close to her? I mean, you were practically hugging!"

Brad just stared at her. "Whoa. Are you jealous?"

Into the Word

Jealousy—another one of those sins that can control our lives so easily. So why is God described as a jealous God?

We get jealous when someone else gets something—or someone—we want. The same is true for God. But while our desire stems from our sinful nature, His comes from His righteous love for His creation.

When God established His covenant with the Israelites during their exodus from Egypt, He marked the Israelites as His own. He reestablished this relationship with various other covenants in the Old Testament, and finally with the new covenant of His Son through Jesus' death and resurrection.

God's covenant is a sign of His love, but His jealousy—His desire for His children to have an exclusive relationship with Him—is also a sign of His love. He doesn't want us to stray from Him, putting other things and other people ahead of Him in our lives. To do so would mean eternal death, and God wants nothing more than to have us with Him in heaven.

In My Life

For us, jealousy usually does more harm than good. No matter what causes it, our jealousy can destroy the relationships and trust we have with one another, and sometimes even the relationship and trust we have with God. When jealousy takes control, we need God's forgiveness, and we also need His help to live jealousy-free, in true and selfless love.

Prayer Thought

Think about those times when jealousy seems to take control of your life and confess them to God. Then trust in Him who has called you His own to forgive you.

As He walked along, He saw Levi son of Alphaeus sitting at the tax collector's booth. "Follow Me," Jesus told Him, and Levi got up and followed Him. While Jesus was having dinner at Levi's house, many tax collectors and "sinners" were eating with Him and His disciples, for there were many who followed Him. *Mark 2:14–15*

Something to Think About

"Hey! Look over there," Rick whispered to the other youth group members sitting near him in church. "Isn't that the new girl who started coming here last month? Does she really think she's going to fit in with us?"

"Yeah," Jen whispered back. "As if she's anything like us. We've been Christians all our lives, but from what I've heard about her, it's obvious she doesn't know a thing about Christianity.

"And look who's with her," Kristi added. "I guess someone forgot to tell her and her friends that leather and chains don't belong in church."

Jen laughed. "Or remember last week? That chick with the Gothic makeup? Who's she going to bring next week?"

Rick just shook his head. "New Christians," he said with a sigh.

Into the Word

Jesus saw Levi sitting at his tax collector's booth and instructed him: "Follow Me." And Levi, without hesitation, got up and followed Jesus.

Then without months of instruction in the faith, or years of growing into Christian maturity, he invited all his friends and associates to his house. He also invited Jesus and His disciples. He did not want to discuss the Roman tax codes or the social position of the notorious "sinners" in the group. He had something much more important in mind.

Levi had found the Messiah, the Savior who loved him and called him to follow in spite of his sinfulness. And he couldn't wait to tell his friends.

In My Life

Sometimes new Christians have the courage to do what "older" Christians don't—share the Good News of Christ with anyone and everyone. They are so excited about the new change wrought in them by the saving grace of Jesus that they simply must share it!

In reality, however, all of us, whether 15 or 50, lifelong Christian or baptized last week, are newly born every day. Through daily repentance and remembrance of the washing and renewal we received in our Baptism, we are made new in Christ.

The only question is: do we act like it?

Prayer

Lord, thank You for making me a new creation. Give me the courage to live each day as Your redeemed child, and help me to share my excitement with others. In Your name I pray. Amen.

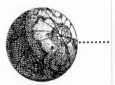

As He looked up, Jesus saw the rich putting their gifts into the treasury. He also saw a poor widow put in two very small copper coins. "I tell you the truth," He said, "this poor widow has put in more than all the others. All these people gave their gifts out of their wealth; but she out of her poverty put in all she had to live on." *Luke 21:1–4*

Something to Think About

The missionary finished his presentation with an impassioned plea for financial support. As the ushers came forward for the offering plates, men and women searched through their wallets and purses for an appropriate offering.

Old Mr. Murphy, the penny-pinching owner of the mill just outside town, pulled a wrinkled dollar bill from his wallet and held it up for the people around him to see. "When I was just a boy," he said, "a missionary came to our church and spoke just like tonight. My heart was moved as he told about preaching the Gospel in far off lands, and I wanted to help with his work. I had a dollar in my pocket that night—all the money I had earned that week delivering groceries—and I put the whole thing in the offering. Since then I have become very successful in business, and I believe it's because that night long ago I gave all I had."

Just then the offering plate came to Mr. Murphy. As he placed his dollar bill in the plate, an old woman in the back of the church challenged, "I dare you to do it again!"

Into the Word

Jesus might have felt the same way about the wealthy people He observed in the temple. Their offerings looked grand in comparison to the two copper coins given by the poor widow. But Jesus knew her gift represented a true sacrifice. She gave all she had to live on.

Jesus, after all, was the expert on sacrificial giving. He gave even more than "all He had to live on." He gave His life itself. On the cross, He became the sacrifice God required to pay for our sins.

In My Life

Because Jesus gave so much for us, we are able to give sacrificially for Him and for others. We can do this when we support His work in proportion to the financial blessings He has given us. We can do this when we use the abilities He has given us to serve the people He has placed around us.

What do you have to give?

Prayer

Lord, You have given me all I have. Thank You for Your blessings. Help me give of myself and the talents You have given me to further Your kingdom. Amen.

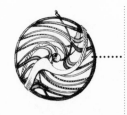

In those days Peter stood up among the believers ... and said, "Brothers, the Scripture had to be fulfilled which the Holy Spirit spoke long ago through the mouth of David concerning Judas, who served as guide for those who arrested Jesus—he was one of our number and shared in this ministry ... Therefore it is necessary to choose one of the men who have been with us the whole time the Lord Jesus went in and out among us, beginning from John's baptism to the time when Jesus was taken up from us. For one of these must become a witness with us of His resurrection." *Acts 1:15–17,21–22*

Into the Word

A big decision faced the disciples. Judas, one of the original twelve disciples, had betrayed Jesus and committed suicide. Now, between the time of Jesus' ascension and the coming of the Holy Spirit on Pentecost, the remaining disciples and other believers needed to choose a replacement for Judas.

Notice how they went about the task. Since Jesus' ascension, the group of believers had been meeting in an upper room in Jerusalem to pray. Their decision-making process grew out of their communication with God in prayer. Before choosing candidates, Peter set out the criteria: the man must have been among Jesus' followers from the beginning of His public ministry—His baptism by John—to the end, when He returned to heaven just a few days earlier. These qualifications would make the new apostle a believable witness to Jesus' resurrection.

The believers proposed two candidates who met the criteria. Lots were cast, and Matthias replaced Judas Iscariot as the twelfth apostle.

In My Life

Do you face an important decision in your life? Perhaps you are deciding on what kind of classes to take in high school. You may have to decide between a job, extra-curricular activities, or more time spent on homework. You may be trying to decide whether to attend college, or which college you should attend.

Whatever the decision, you can learn a lot from the disciples' example. They approached decision-making with an attitude of prayer, seeking God's guidance in each decision and in all other matters in their lives. They set criteria for possible choices—criteria consistent with God's Word. Then they asked God to help them make the right choice.

For us today, decision-making can happen the same way. Pray about your choices, asking God to guide and bless your decision. Then rest assured in faith that He has heard your prayer and will lead you on the path He has chosen.

Prayer

Lord, You chose me to be Your child, and redeemed me through Jesus' death and resurrection. Help me in all the choices that face me, that my choices may always be pleasing to You. Amen.

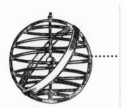

My frame was not hidden from You when I was made in the secret place. When I was woven together in the depths of the earth, Your eyes saw my unformed body. All the days ordained for me were written in Your book before one of them came to be. *Psalm 139:15–16*

Something to Think About

"Hey, Karla," Jen said, coming up to her friend just as she was shutting her locker. "Can I talk to you about something? Just between us?"

Karla glanced around the empty hallway. "Sure. What's up?"

"What do you think about abortion?"

Karla laughed uncomfortably. "Okay—that's out of nowhere."

"Just tell me what you think." Jen tried not to sound desperate.

"Well—" Karla paused. "It's a choice. I mean, all the pro-lifers say it's a baby, but I don't think so. The fetus can't even live on its own until maybe six months. No, it's my body and my mom has always told me I have the right to choose what happens with my body, so I guess that means I'm all for it." She paused. "Why?"

Jen glanced around the hall, making sure they really were alone. "Because I'm pregnant."

Into the Word

The writer of Psalm 139 offers a description of intrauterine life that's not found in science books: "My frame was not hidden from You when I was made in the secret place (the womb) ... Your eyes saw my unformed body." Not only saw me, but knew me, made plans for me, ordained the number of my days, loved me as one redeemed by His Son.

Fearfully and wonderfully made—the creation of a loving, all-knowing God. That's true of every fetus and every baby. Each one has a soul for which Jesus suffered and died. The only difference between them is time.

In My Life

Pregnancy is never easy or without risk. It is especially difficult when the mother is very young, very old, unmarried, married to another person, already burdened with several children, still in high school or college, or financially unable to care for a child. The choice to overcome these and other problems is a very difficult one for any prospective mother and father.

But life is a gift from God. Celebrate life, and praise Him.

Prayer

Forgive us, Lord, for trampling on the rights of the unborn. Help those faced with unplanned pregnancies to seek solutions other than abortion. Amen.

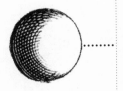

Then Jesus said to them, "Give to Caesar what is Caesar's and to God what is God's." *Mark 12:17*

Into the Word

Those sly foxes, the Pharisees and the Herodians, knew they had Jesus this time. No matter how He answered, He would be in trouble. After their opening flattery, they got to the question: "Is it right to pay taxes to Caesar or not?" Answer no, and He would be arrested by the Romans; answer yes, and He would be killed by the Jewish mob, who hated the tax, which denoted Roman authority.

Jesus knew exactly what they were doing. "Bring me a denarius and let me look at it," He said. The denarius, worth about one day's wages, had on one side a picture of the Emperor Tiberius and on the other the inscription, "Tiberius Caesar Augustus, son of the divine Augustus." The coin was issued by Caesar and was used for paying taxes to him. "Whose portrait is this? And whose inscription?" asked Jesus.

"Caesar's," they replied.

Jesus concluded, "Give to Caesar what is Caesar's and to God what is God's."

In My Life

The denarius bore the image of Tiberius Caesar Augustus. It had been issued by him, belonged to him, and, as the coin used for taxes, it was to be returned to him.

In the beginning, the writer of Genesis tells us, "God created man in His own image" (Genesis 1:27). God made Adam and Eve in His image: holy, perfect, sinless. They bore His image, as the denarius bore Caesar's. When God's image was lost through sin, God sent His Son to redeem the people He had created. Through Jesus' death in our place, God's image has been restored to us. We belong to Him.

As the Jews were to give back to Caesar the coin that bore his image, so we are to give to God that which bears His image. "Therefore I urge you, brothers, in view of God's mercy, to offer your bodies as living sacrifices, holy and pleasing to God—this is your spiritual act of worship" (Romans 12:1).

Prayer

Take my life, O Lord, renew,
Consecrate my heart to You;
Take my moments and my days;
Let them sing Your ceaseless praise.
Take my love; my Lord, I pour
At Your feet its treasure store;
Take my self, Lord, let me be
Yours alone eternally. Amen.
(*Lutheran Worship*, #404)

Peter said to Him, "We have left all we had to follow You!"

"I tell you the truth," Jesus said to them, "no one who has left home or wife or brothers or parents or children for the sake of the kingdom of God will fail to receive many times as much in this age and, in the age to come, eternal life." *Luke 18:28–30*

Something to Think About

The history of the United States is filled with stories of the immigrants who came to America to begin a new life. Whether they had been rich or poor in their native lands, almost all of them left behind their possessions or converted them to cash to pay for the journey. They also said good-bye to friends and relatives they were not likely to see again.

What motivated them to come? Some sought religious freedom; some freedom from political oppression. The majority, however, wanted a better life, the opportunity to make a fortune for themselves and their children. The promise of better days to come sustained many immigrant families through the poverty and homesickness of their first years in America.

Into the Word

Peter spoke for all the disciples: "We have left all we had to follow You!" Perhaps he had been thinking about the fishing boat in Galilee or his wife and family in Capernaum. The other disciples must have nodded in agreement, remembering homes and friends they hadn't seen for many months.

Jesus knew their thoughts and reassured them with this promise: "No one who has left home or wife or brothers or parents or children for the sake of the kingdom of God will fail to receive many times as much in this age and, in the age to come, eternal life" (Luke 18:29–30).

In My Life

What have you been asked to give up to follow Jesus?

Do some of your friends avoid you because you go to church? Jesus promises to always be with you. Has your conscience forced you to repent of and give up popular but sinful activities? Jesus promises to forgive your sins and free you from sin's control. Does your family think you're weird for taking your faith so seriously? Jesus promises you the love and support of the family of God.

And, in the age to come, He promises to give you eternal life.

Prayer

Lord Jesus, give me the faith to follow You, no matter what the cost. In Your name I pray. Amen.

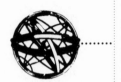

"My prayer is not that You take them out of the world but that You protect them from the evil one. They are not of the world, even as I am not of it. Sanctify them by the truth; Your Word is truth. As You sent Me into the world, I have sent them into the world." *John 17:15–18*

Something to Think About

Anna and Susan sat on Susan's family room floor watching TV and talking about the party they planned to go to Saturday night. "All I know is my mom said if I miss my curfew one more time, she and my dad are sending me to a convent!" Susan rolled her eyes.

"Are they serious?" asked Anna. "Would they really do that?"

"I don't think so," said Susan, not quite sure, "but you can bet I'll be home on time this week, just in case." She thought quietly for a minute and then said, "You know, Anna, sometimes life in a convent sounds like a relief. So much less to deal with: Bob wouldn't be pushing a beer into my face at every party; Dana wouldn't be asking me to smoke with her at lunch; Jim wouldn't be pushing me to go too far; people wouldn't put me down because I go to church or because I listen to my parents … Maybe a convent is where a Christian belongs."

Into the Word

Jesus often warned His disciples that the world would hate them just as it had hated Him. On the night before He died, Jesus prayed for His disciples. He could have asked His Father to protect them by removing them from the world; instead He asked God to leave them in the world, but protect them from the power of the devil.

Because they belonged to Him and not the world, Jesus knew His disciples would never fit into the culture around them. He prayed for the Holy Spirit to sanctify them, to make them holy through God's Word.

Jesus had come into the world on a mission—to bring salvation to all people through His death on the cross. His disciples too had a mission while they were in the world—to bring the Good News of salvation to everyone, so that they too might believe and be saved.

In My Life

The next time you're ready to yell, "Stop the world! I want to get off!" remember *your* mission. It's the reason Jesus wants you here. And remember, His prayer for His disciples is His prayer for you: "My prayer is not that You take them out of the world but that You protect them from the evil one."

Prayer

Protect me, Lord, from the power of the devil, and empower me through Your Word for my mission here in the world. Amen.

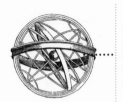

There are different kinds of gifts, but the same Spirit. There are different kinds of service, but the same Lord. There are different kinds of working, but the same God works all of them in all men.
1 Corinthians 12:4–6

Something to Think About

"Okay, guys," David shouted above the noise of the youth group, "Quiet down. We have to plan out the youth service we'll be doing in a couple weeks."

Cathy felt her stomach drop at the thought of the service. She shot Heidi a look of terror before turning to face David.

He stood at the front of the room, clipboard in hand. "Does anyone have anything they *want* to do? We need people to act in the skits, probably some people to help them find props and costumes too. We need readers for the Scripture passages. We need music—maybe we could form a choir?" David looked up, but several people just groaned. "Okay, so not all of you. We need people to work on the bulletin, ushers ... Does anything sound interesting?"

Ellie raised her hand. "I'll help with the music."

"Dan and I will help you with the skits if we can get some more people to act," Joseph said, glancing around to make sure others would help him.

"What do you want to do?" Heidi whispered to Cathy.

Cathy shook her head. "I don't know. I don't think I can do any of this stuff."

"Me either. Do you want to pretend we have something else to do that weekend?"

"No, I really want to help," Cathy sighed. "I just wish I could sing or act."

In My Life

Knowing what Jesus has done for us—dying to free us from sin and death—makes us want to serve Him. But how shall we serve?

You may want to do big, important things for Him because your love for Him is great. But you may think that you are too young or live too far away or don't have the talents or training needed to do what you want.

Don't give up. Look at the talents God has given you. They will probably be different from the talents of your friends or family members, but you do have them. Then look at what needs to be done where He has put you. You don't have to do big things. If the small things you do for others are motivated by what Jesus did for you, they will reflect His love. In that reflection people will see your Savior and will want to know Him too.

Think of some ways you can serve Him this week, right where you are.

Prayer

Lord Jesus, You have done so much for me, even giving Your life to save me. Show me how to serve others so they see Your love in me. Amen.

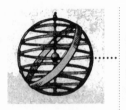

"Woe to the world because of the things that cause people to sin! Such things must come, but woe to the man through whom they come!"
Matthew 18:7

Something to Think About

Brad could hardly wait for Friday night to come. Jeff had invited everybody who was anybody to his graduation party—the whole football team, the cheerleaders, the group from the ski club. Although Brad was only a sophomore, he knew a lot of people from student council and the newspaper. Still, he couldn't believe Jeff had included him.

On Tuesday before the party Jeff stopped Brad in the hall. "By the way, Brad," he said casually, "just figure on staying overnight Friday at my house. My mom and dad said if anybody gets in trouble on the way home from the party, they'd be responsible, since they're buying the beer. My mom says you all better sleep on the floor and go home in the morning."

"Sure, no problem," Brad mumbled as Jeff walked over to talk to another group of kids. But after Jeff left, Brad stood and thought for a long time about what to do.

Into the Word

Temptation. It's not a sin, but it's always trying to lead you there. "Try it; you'll like it!" "It can't be wrong if it feels good." "Everybody's doing it!" "You have to look out for number one."

If it's any consolation, you're not alone. Everyone who has ever lived has had to deal with temptation—even Jesus! To learn how the devil tempted Him and how He handled it, read Matthew 4:1–11. And it always follows the same old patterns. Paul wrote, "No temptation has seized you except what is common to man" (1 Corinthians 10:13a).

Paul also provides the way out. "God is faithful," Paul promises; "He will not let you be tempted beyond what you can bear. But when you are tempted, He will also provide a way out so that you can stand up under it" (1 Corinthians 10:13b).

In My Life

The next time you are tempted, look for the way out. Close the textbook left open during the exam. Don't bring your date home when your parents are gone. Stay home from the party where you know alcohol and drugs will be available. The same Jesus who died to forgive your sins will help you resist the temptation to keep on sinning.

Prayer Idea

When you go to Jesus for forgiveness, ask Him to help you find a way out of temptation.

Then Peter said, "Silver or gold I do not have, but what I have I give you. In the name of Jesus Christ of Nazareth, walk." Taking him by the right hand, he helped him up, and instantly the man's feet and ankles became strong. *Acts 3:6–7*

Something to Think About

It always embarrassed Jim to ask, but he had no other choice. "Mr. Swanson," he said to Eric's dad, "my parents have to go away this weekend and won't be able to drive me to the swim meet. Could I please get a ride with you and your family?"

Jim was packed and ready when the Swansons picked him up Saturday morning. On the way to the meet, Eric shared the gigantic lunch Mrs. Swanson had packed for the two boys. Whenever Jim competed in a race, he could hear Mr. and Mrs. Swanson cheering for him, just as they cheered for Eric. After the meet, Mr. Swanson took them all to a nice restaurant and insisted on paying for Jim's dinner.

When the Swansons' car pulled up in front of Jim's house, he thanked the family for all they had done. "I only asked you for a ride to the meet," said Jim, "but you did much more for me."

Into the Word

When the crippled beggar who always sat at the temple gate asked Peter and John for money, a few coins was the best he expected to receive. But Peter, through the power of the risen Christ, gave the man what he really needed most. Taking him by his hand, Peter helped him to his feet. Instantly the crippled feet and ankles became strong.

In My Life

We take our troubles and concerns to God in prayer asking Him to give us what we think we need. But God knows our needs much better than we do, and He responds by giving us much more than we asked.

We ask Him to make us well when we are sick, and He heals us from the spiritual sickness of sin. We ask Him for food for our bodies and He also feeds our souls through His Word and sacraments.

We ask for relief from the guilt of sin and He wipes out all of our sins for the sake of Jesus, who died that we might be forgiven.

We ask for His care during our life on earth. He does this, and in addition to this and everything else, He promises us a joyful eternity with Him in heaven.

Prayer

Almighty God, Your generosity and power are beyond my wildest imagination. Help me to trust You to always provide exactly what I need for this life and the next. Amen.

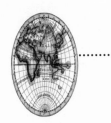

I will come to Your temple with burnt offerings and fulfill my vows to You—vows my lips promised and my mouth spoke when I was in trouble. Psalm 66:13–14

Something to Think About

Ramon and Terry clung to their over-turned boat and trembled with cold. "I haven't done real well up to now, God," Ramon prayed aloud, "but if You send someone to rescue us, I'll never miss church again in my whole life."

Over the roar of the wind and waves, the boys heard the sound of a motor. In less than half an hour, they sat huddled in blankets, holding mugs of hot coffee on a Coast Guard search-and-rescue boat headed for shore. "You're really lucky we found you," said the sailor who had pulled Ramon from the water. "A fisherman called and told us he thought he had seen a small boat over-turn." Ramon looked at Terry and smiled. He knew it was more than luck.

The telephone woke Ramon at 9:00 the next morning. "Do you want my parents to pick you up on the way to church, Ramon?" asked Terry.

"Church?" asked Ramon sleepily. Then he remembered. "Maybe I'll start that next Sunday."

Into the Word

Hannah prayed for a son and promised to give him back to God. God answered her prayer. When Samuel was still very young, she and Elkanah took him to the house of the Lord at Shiloh, where they dedicated him to God's service for the rest of his life. (1 Samuel 1:1–2:11)

From deep inside the belly of the fish, Jonah prayed for rescue. He vowed to worship God with songs of thanksgiving and sacrifice. God caused the fish to vomit Jonah onto dry land. And Jonah obeyed God's command and went to Nineveh to preach repentance. (Jonah 2–3)

In My Life

Have you made any promises to God? Perhaps you, like Ramon, have promised in panic, offering God anything on the spur of the moment to get you out of a bad situation. Did you, like Ramon, forget about your promise once your feet were on dry ground?

Or was your promise more deliberate, something you'd planned and thought about? If you have been confirmed, you have promised to be faithful to God for the rest of your life. But even after a lot of thought, it is still easy to forget about your promise, isn't it?

Why is it so important to keep our promises to God? Because He kept His promise to us when He sent His Son, Jesus, to be our Savior. Through Jesus, we have the power to keep our vows to God.

Prayer

Forgive me, Lord, for taking lightly the promises I've made to You. Thank You for never forgetting Your promises to me. Amen.

Praise the LORD, O my soul; all my inmost being, praise His holy name. Praise the LORD, O my soul, and forget not all His benefits.
Psalm 103:1-2

Into the Word

Find and read the complete text of Psalm 103 in your Bible. In this psalm, David praises God for all that He has done for His people, Israel.

Notice the form of the psalm. Verses 1–2 and verses 20–22 frame the rest of the psalm like a pair of bookends, stating the theme of the psalm: that everyone and everything should praise the Lord. The main body of the psalm has two parts. Verses 3–5 tell of the benefits David has received personally. Verses 6–19 recount God's blessings to His people.

Even the number of verses is significant—there is one verse for each of the 22 letters in the Hebrew alphabet. You can find other examples of this in Psalms 33 and 34.

In My Life

If you were the writer of Psalm 103, which of God's benefits would you include? What are your top ten reasons to praise God?

10. _____

9. _____

8. _____

7. _____

6. _____

5. _____

4. _____

3. _____

2. _____

1. _____

What did you choose as your number one reason to praise God? Of all of His benefits, which is most important to you?

You can find which one Paul would have chosen as number one by reading what he wrote to the Roman Christians: "He who did not spare His own Son, but gave Him up for us all—how will He not also, along with Him, graciously give us all things?" (Romans 8:32). To Paul, the fact that God had given us His Son to be our Savior guaranteed that He would also provide everything else we would ever need.

Prayer Thought

Make up a prayer of praise and thanksgiving to God for all His benefits. Use your personal top ten list to help you remember them.

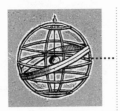

But Peter and John replied, "Judge for yourselves whether it is right in God's sight to obey you rather than God. For we cannot help speaking about what we have seen and heard." *Acts 4:19–20*

Something to Think About

Have you ever witnessed something really exciting? Perhaps it was a basketball game decided by a half-court shot at the closing buzzer. Or maybe the rescue of someone trapped in an overturned car. Whatever the event, you probably couldn't wait to tell someone about it. Not just once, but over and over you told what you had seen.

Now imagine that you were the person who was rescued. You wouldn't be able to stop telling about the wonderful deed of the one who had saved you. And each time you told the story, you would feel even more grateful to your rescuer.

Into the Word

Peter and John were in a spot. On the one hand, the Sanhedrin, the ruling religious council in Jerusalem, had ordered them to stop preaching and teaching in the name of Jesus. They had already spent one night in jail, and the Sanhedrin's threats sounded ominous.

But, on the other hand, they had witnessed the greatest rescue in history. For three years they had followed Jesus, the Son of God, as He carried on His earthly ministry. They had witnessed His crucifixion and His resurrection. And they couldn't help telling what they had seen and heard.

In My Life

You and I also witnessed that rescue—through the Word of God. We recognize ourselves among the sinners Jesus died to save. How can we keep from telling what we have seen and heard?

Excited about the rescue, we share the Good News with others that they too have been saved by Jesus' death on the cross. In doing this, we join the witnesses Jesus commissioned before He ascended into heaven to carry the Gospel to everyone on earth. With whom could you share this Good News?

Prayer

Jesus, You have done so much for me—even dying to take away my sins. Help me to tell and retell this Good News until everyone has heard. Amen.

"A farmer went out to sow his seed. As he was scattering the seed, some fell along the path, and the birds came and ate it up. Some fell on rocky places ... Other seed fell among thorns ... Still other seed fell on good soil, where it produced a crop—a hundred, sixty or thirty times what was sown."
Matthew 13:3-9

In My Life

Dear Pastor,

You know how excited I've been about knowing Jesus as my Savior since our youth retreat last summer, and I wish all my friends could know the happiness I've found in Jesus.

But I seem to have run into a problem. I've told three of my friends what Jesus means to me and how He's changed my life. Then I invited them to come with me to youth group or to church. One said she wouldn't be ready to commit to a formal religion until she was older. Another one came once, but now seems to be avoiding me so I haven't invited her again. The third friend said he'd come, but then he called to say something else had come up that he had to do instead.

What's wrong with me? Can you tell me what am I doing wrong?

Discouraged

Into the Word

Dear Discouraged,

Jesus told a parable that sounds like your letter. He compared the Word of God to seed being scattered by a farmer. All of the seed was good seed. But not all of it grew into healthy plants.

Some seeds fell along the path; nothing grew where many feet tramped every day. The path wasn't ready for seeds, just as your first friend wasn't ready for the Gospel. Other seeds fell on rocky ground; they germinated in the shallow soil but couldn't maintain their growth. This sounds like your second friend. Still other seeds fell among thorns and were choked out by the fast-growing weeds. Your third friend's interest in the Gospel was choked out by other demands in his life.

It was the farmer's job to sow the seeds, but the farmer had no power at all to make the seeds grow. Witnessing is a lot like that—you can tell people about Jesus, but you can't make anyone believe in Him. Faith comes through the power of the Holy Spirit. And when the Spirit works faith in hearts where you have sown God's Word, a plentiful crop of Christians will result.

Pastor

Prayer

Keep me from getting discouraged, Lord, when I don't see the results of my witness for You. Send Your Holy Spirit to bring faith to hearts that have heard Your Word, and make me a persistent witness. Amen.

"But he answered one of them, 'Friend, I am not being unfair to you. Didn't you agree to work for a denarius? Take your pay and go. I want to give the man who was hired last the same as I gave you. Don't I have the right to do what I want with my own money? Or are you envious because I am generous?'

"So the last will be first, and the first will be last." *Matthew 20:13–16*

Something to Think About

Who do you expect to see in heaven? The people from your church (at least the ones that come every week and sit up front)? Your pastors and youth group leaders? The preachers you see on TV? Would you expect to see a thief? Someone who claimed he didn't even know Jesus? Someone known for killing Christians?

Into the Word

Jesus told a parable about a landowner who went out early in the morning to hire laborers for his vineyard. He agreed to pay them a denarius a day, and they went to work. At 9:00 A.M. he hired more laborers, telling them he would pay them whatever was right. The same thing happened at noon and again at 3:00 P.M. At 5:00 P.M., he found more laborers without work, so he hired them too.

In the evening, the owner told his foreman to pay the laborers, beginning with the ones who were hired last. Each worker received a denarius. When the foreman got to the laborers who had worked all day, they expected to receive more. But each received the denarius he had been promised. "These men who were hired last worked only one hour," they said, "and you have made them equal to us who have borne the burden of the work and the heat of the day."

The owner answered, "Friend, I am not being unfair to you. Didn't you agree to work for a denarius? ... Don't I have the right to do what I want with my own money? Or are you envious because I am generous?" (Matthew 20:13,15)

Jesus used the parable to teach the disciples a lesson about God's grace, which He gives freely and generously to all who believe. Lifelong Christians and deathbed converts alike are saved by grace, not length of service.

In My Life

Are you envious because God is generous to the last-minute Christian? Instead, thank Him for His marvelous generosity to you.

(To identify the thief, the person who denied Christ, and the persecutor you'll meet in heaven, read Luke 23:39–43, Luke 22:54–62, and Acts 9:1–2.)

Prayer

Forgive me, Lord, for acting as though I deserve a place in heaven. Thank You for saving me by grace through the death of Jesus Christ. Amen.

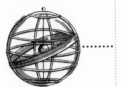

What then shall we say? That the Gentiles, who did not pursue righteousness, have obtained it, a righteousness that is by faith; but Israel, who pursued a law of righteousness, has not attained it. Why not? Because they pursued it not by faith but as if it were by works. They stumbled over the "stumbling stone." *Romans 9:30–32*

Something to Think About

"*Antidisestablishmentarianism* is the longest word in the English language. Can you spell it?"

When you were a child, were you ever tricked by this riddle? Most children will wrinkle their foreheads, calling out names of letters, starting over again and again, trying to spell the long word—never realizing the riddle really asks them to spell the tiny word *it*. Their fascination with the long word and their enthusiasm for the challenge of spelling it serve as stumbling blocks to accomplishing the real task.

Into the Word

Paul explained the plight of the Jews in similar terms. God had given His Law to the Jewish people on Mt. Sinai. The Law showed the people how God intended for them to live. Because the Law reflected God's own holiness, it would show the children of Israel their sin and point them in faith to the Savior God would send for them.

But the Jews tried to make keeping the Law the way to become righteous. They took great pride in keeping each sentence of the ceremonial laws as recorded in the books of Moses. In addition they carefully observed volumes of traditions established by the rabbis. Surely, they believed, God would declare them righteous for their efforts. Surely He would judge the Gentiles, who did not keep the Law, as unworthy.

But Paul says that the Law itself became a stumbling block to the Jews. It was not that they pursued the wrong goal—righteousness before God—but that they pursued it the wrong way, by their own efforts to keep the Law. In their single-minded emphasis on keeping the Law, the Jews rejected God's means of salvation—by grace through faith in Jesus Christ.

In My Life

It is easy for us today to still get caught up in the Law, or the things we have to do. When we think we have to be a good Christian, to make God like us or to "earn" salvation, the task at hand can overcome us. But here's good news: God says we are completely righteous not because of anything we have done, but because of what Jesus, His righteous Son, has done for us.

Prayer

Jesus, I've done so many things wrong. But in faith I can stand before God, knowing He will judge me righteous because of You. Amen.

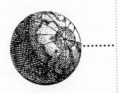

The kings of the earth take their stand and the rulers gather together against the LORD and against His Anointed One. "Let us break their chains," they say, "and throw off their fetters." *Psalm 2:2–3*

Something to Think About

"I can't stand being treated like a slave!" Gina shouted to her parents. "I'm sick of your rules and your religion. I need my freedom!" And Gina ran away.

Six months later, Gina was arrested in New York for prostitution. On her face was a bright red scar, the result of a knife wound from her pimp. And needle tracks on her arm showed evidence of heroin addiction. Gina was 15 years old.

Into the Word

Gina understood what the psalmist meant about "breaking chains" and "throwing off fetters." Rebellion against authority is as old as sin itself, and it's not limited to youth. It is a result of the first sin in the Garden of Eden, when Adam and Eve wanted to do things their way instead of God's.

Look what happened to Adam and Eve. They traded one kind of "slavery" for another. Instead of obeying the loving Creator, who provided them with everything they needed, they were now slaves to sin and all it entailed: pain and suffering, endless labor, family problems, separation from God, and finally death. And as Adam and Eve's descendants, we were born into slavery.

But in our desperate condition, God loved us and planned to free us. He sent His only Son to take our place, to carry our sins to the cross and die for them there. As Jesus broke free from the grave Easter morning, so we, through faith in Him, have thrown off the shackles of our bondage.

In My Life

Since God's Son has set us free, we no longer live as slaves. Instead of being bound by old sinful habits, we are free to serve God and live in harmony with our neighbor. Instead of selfishly turning inward, thinking first of our own desires and pleasures, we are free to love and praise God with all our hearts. No longer entangled in old habits of rebellion, we can love our parents, teachers, and others in authority and show them the respect due them. Free from jealousy and anger, we can forgive, support, and encourage both friends and enemies.

After all, that's what Jesus has done for us.

Prayer

Lord, forgive my sins for the sake of Jesus, who died to make me free. Then help me use my freedom to live for You. Amen.

John's disciples told Him about all these things. Calling two of them, he sent them to the Lord to ask, "Are You the One who was to come, or should we expect someone else?" At that very time Jesus cured many who had diseases, sicknesses, and evil spirits, and gave sight to many who were blind. So He replied to the messengers, "Go back and report to John what you have seen and heard: The blind receive sight, the lame walk, those who have leprosy are cured, the deaf hear, the dead are raised, and the good news is preached to the poor. Blessed is the man who does not fall away on account of Me." *Luke 7:18–19,21–23*

Something to Think About

"I don't understand what's wrong with me," confessed Joel. "Sometimes my faith is so strong I could fight off the devil himself. But other times I have many questions and even doubts. What can I do?"

"Doubts?" asked Janie. "How can you be a Christian if you have doubts? Your faith must really be in danger."

Into the Word

John the Baptist had his doubts. He seemed unflappable, out there in the desert, baptizing in the river and calling the Jews to repent—so sure when he pointed to his cousin, Jesus, as the Lamb of God. Now the spotlight had shifted from John to Jesus and John received only incomplete reports about Jesus' work: hillside sermons to thousands of listeners, messages of love and forgiveness, a centurion's servant healed, a widow's son brought back from the dead. Who was this Jesus? What if John had been wrong?

So John sent two of his disciples to find out. Jesus didn't belittle John for his questions or make light of his doubt. Instead He answered John's questions: the blind see, the lame walk, those who have leprosy are cured, the deaf hear, the dead are raised, and the good news is preached to the poor. In other words, Jesus had done exactly what the Messiah was supposed to do.

In My Life

Don't worry about the condition of your faith when you have questions. Instead, do what John did, go to the source of information, the Word of God. Ask your pastor, youth leader, or Christian friends to help you find the answers. Jesus didn't want doubt or discouragement to keep John from knowing Him as his Savior from sin. He cares just as much about you.

Prayer

I believe, Lord, but I have so many questions. Send Your Holy Spirit to help me understand Your Word, and make my faith strong. In Jesus' name. Amen.

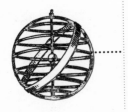

For I am about to fall, and my pain is ever with me. I confess my iniquity; I am troubled by my sin. *Psalm 38:17–18*

Something to Think About

When hiking back country trails in the Rocky Mountains, it is often necessary to cross streams on log bridges. These single logs, anchored between boulders on either side of the stream for stability, sometimes come equipped with hand rails and sometimes don't. While these picturesque bridges provide little challenge for agile hikers, for a klutz, they guarantee disaster. The question is never "if" there will be a fall, it's "when." An unbalanced backpack may shift its weight to one side or a bird's call may break one's concentration. Regardless, the more a hiker thinks about the stream beneath the log bridge, the quicker he or she will end up in it.

Into the Word

The psalmist is afraid of falling too— falling into death. He has become so weakened by his spiritual and physical problems that he has lost all hope. "My guilt has overwhelmed me like a burden too heavy to bear," he writes. "My back is filled with searing pain; there is no health in my body. I am feeble and utterly crushed; I groan in anguish of heart" (Psalm 38:4, 7–8).

With what seems like his last breath, he calls on God to help him. "O Lord, do not forsake me; be not far from me, O my God. Come quickly to help me, O Lord my Savior" (Psalm 38:21-22).

It is almost as if he was crossing a log bridge and slipped under the weight of his problems. Now he hangs on desperately to the log, his last hope before being swept away to his death.

In My Life

Sometimes the only way to get yourself safely across a log bridge is to focus your attention on something solid on the other side. But the only way to avoid eternal death is to focus on Jesus and His saving grace. If we lose sight of Him and begin concentrating on the troubles and sins that weigh us down, we slip and fall.

Our best efforts to stay focused often fail. When they do, we should pray as the psalmist did: "I confess my iniquity; I am troubled by my sin.... Come quickly to help me, O Lord my Savior" (Psalm 38:18, 22). Then all we need to do is trust He has forgiven us and will help us, no matter how close to death we think we are.

Prayer

Lord God, I always seem to be slipping and falling. Forgive me for focusing on everything but You. Come quickly to help me, and keep me steady on Your path. In Your name, Amen.

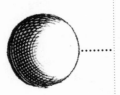

When they came to the place called the Skull, there they crucified Him, along with the criminals—one on His right, the other on His left. Jesus said, "Father, forgive them, for they do not know what they are doing."
Luke 23:33–34

Something to Think About

In the center of the city of Coventry, in the United Kingdom, the spire and ruined shell of an old cathedral stand, open to the sky, next to a modern brick church dedicated in 1962. The old cathedral, built in the 1300s, was destroyed by a German air raid in 1940 that devastated most of the central city and killed many civilians. Where its altar once stood, today an altar made of rubble bears these words: "Father, forgive."

Since World War II, the Coventry Cathedral has been the center of the Reconciliation Movement. Originally organized to bring reconciliation between the people of the United Kingdom and Germany through forgiveness, its emphasis has now widened to include countries and altercations around the world.

Into the Word

From the cross Jesus prayed, "Father, forgive," asking God to forgive the people who were killing Him. His words brought reconciliation with God to the people who witnessed His death. The dying thief turned to Jesus in faith and was assured of paradise. The centurion proclaimed, "Surely He was the Son of God!" (Matthew 27:54). And in the days following Jesus' resurrection and ascension, "a large number of priests became obedient to the faith" (Acts 6:7).

In My Life

But the people who nailed Jesus to the cross and witnessed His death weren't the only ones responsible for it. He carried to the cross the sins of everyone who ever lived, including you and me. On the cross, He was punished in our place; He died the death we deserved. And now we bear the righteousness that He gained.

Jesus' words of forgiveness for those who killed Him, then, are spoken directly to us. "Father, forgive _____"(put your own name in the blank). It was for us that He died; for His sake, we are forgiven. By His death we are reconciled with God.

Prayer

There stands a fountain where for sin
Immanuel was slain,
And sinners who are washed therein
Are cleansed from ev'ry stain.
The dying thief rejoiced to see
That fountain in his day;
And there have I, as vile as he,
Washed all my sins away.
Dear dying Lamb, thy precious blood
Shall never lose its pow'r
Till all the ransomed Church of God
Be saved to sin no more. Amen.
(*Lutheran Worship*, stanzas 1–3, #506)

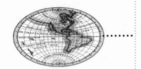

Then James and John, the sons of Zebedee, came to Him. "Teacher," they said, "we want You to do for us whatever we ask." "What do you want Me to do for you?" He asked. They replied, "Let one of us sit at Your right and the other at Your left in Your glory." *Mark 10:35-37*

It was the third hour when they crucified Him. The written notice of the charge against Him read: The King of the Jews. They crucified two robbers with Him, one on His right and one on His left." *Mark 15:25-28*

Into the Word

Those arrogant sons of Zebedee! Planning ahead for the coming of Jesus' kingdom was one thing, but demanding to sit at His right and left hands—places of prestige—was something else.

Jesus answered them with a question. "Can you drink the cup I drink or be baptized with the baptism I am baptized with?" (Mark 10:38). Jesus wanted them to consider whether they would be willing to share what He would soon face, experiencing the wrath of God against sin when He punished His own Son for the sake of sinful mankind.

Did John remember his question that day on Calvary as He watched his Master die? "King of the Jews," the placard read, but this was not the kingdom John had imagined. And the men on His right and left were common criminals also sentenced to death by crucifixion.

In My Life

Through the power of the Holy Spirit, we understand and believe that Jesus died for those two criminals, for James and John, and for you and me. His death was the punishment we deserved for our sins. In His righteousness, we now stand redeemed before God.

Jesus still calls us to drink the cup He drank and be baptized with the Baptism with which He was baptized. In his book, *The Cost of Discipleship*, theologian Dietrich Bonhoeffer suggests that Jesus' call to follow Him is a call to "come and die." Not for the sins of the world—Jesus has already done that once and for all. But He calls us to die to our old way of living, where we put our pleasures and comfort and desires first and the welfare of our neighbor last, if at all.

As Jesus explained to James and John: "Whoever wants to become great among you must be your servant, and whoever wants to be first must be slave of all. For even the Son of Man did not come to be served, but to serve, and to give His life as a ransom for many" (Mark 10:43–45).

Prayer Thought

Ask God to help you remember what's important in the kingdom of God.

While Jesus was having dinner at Matthew's house, many tax collectors and "sinners" came and ate with Him and His disciples. When the Pharisees saw this, they asked His disciples, "Why does your Teacher eat with tax collectors and 'sinners'?"

On hearing this, Jesus said, "It is not the healthy who need a doctor, but the sick. But go and learn what this means: 'I desire mercy, not sacrifice. For I have not come to call the righteous, but sinners.'"

Matthew 9:10–13

Something to Think About

I'm sure you know someone like Linda in your school. "Wild," your friends call her, then repeat the stories going around school about her. Her too-black hair and nails, her strange clothes, the fake gems in her nose and lip, her surly, defiant attitude make every one of the stories easy to believe.

Your parents, of course, warn you about people like Linda. "Trouble," they say, "and if you associate with her, you're headed for trouble too."

You really only see her in the classes you have together or slouching with her friends at the end of the hall during lunch period. But one thing about Linda won't leave your mind—her eyes. Something—is it fear or hurt or vulnerability?—lies behind the hate and rebellion Linda tries to show.

Into the Word

Jesus had gone to Matthew's house to have dinner with the tax collectors and "sinners" that all good Jews found so loathsome. The religious leaders of Jesus' day, the Pharisees, thought they needed to warn Him about keeping company with lowlife types like Matthew. Surely, the Pharisees thought, Jesus would take their warning in a positive manner, knowing they had His own good reputation in mind.

But Jesus' answer infuriated them. "It is not the healthy who need a doctor, but the sick … For I have not come to call the righteous, but sinners" (Matthew 9:12–13).

In My Life

Sinners, Jesus said. If any of the stories about Linda are true, she certainly qualifies. Can't you just see her there at Matthew's house with the prostitutes, the cheaters, and other "lowlifes" at whom the Pharisees looked down their long noses? Can you see the fear and sadness in her eyes change to trust and joy as Jesus tells her how much He loves her?

After all, Jesus came into the world for one reason—to die to save sinners. Like Linda. Like me.

Prayer Thought

Have you looked down on someone because of his or her sin? If so, confess your own sin to Jesus. Thank Him for dying to pay for the sins of all sinners. Then ask Him to help you show His love to the person you thought unworthy.

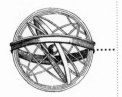

O LORD my God, if I have done this and there is guilt on my hands—if I have done evil to him who is at peace with me or without cause have robbed my foe—then let my enemy pursue and overtake me; let him trample my life to the ground and make me sleep in the dust. Arise, O LORD, in Your anger; rise up against the rage of my enemies. Awake, my God; decree justice.
Psalm 7:3–6

Something to Think About

Ben sat on the locker-room bench, head in hands. He couldn't believe what had happened. Gary had stood there and lied to the coach and the team—and everyone believed him! Now the whole team thought Ben had been drinking at the party, and soon his parents would hear about it too.

Ben didn't understand. How could they believe he'd do something so stupid? How could Gary lie about it? How could he convince the coach—and his parents—that he didn't have anything to drink?

Suddenly, the locker-room door slammed shut. Someone else had come in, and Ben recognized the voice singing on the other side of the lockers. Gary obviously thought Ben would be long gone by now, or else he would not have come down here alone. Not after everything he had done.

Ben rose, slowly and silently. Here was his chance to get even. What could he do?

Into the Word

David might have asked himself a similar question. Enraged by people who said David was trying to kill him, King Saul had led an army of

3,000 men against David's small band into the wilderness of En Gedi. And now it appeared the Lord had led Saul right into David's lap. While searching for David, King Saul went into a cave to go to the bathroom, not realizing that this was the cave in which David and his men were hiding. The opportunity for revenge was ripe, and David's men urged him to get even. However, David followed advice from a higher source.

Instead of taking matters into his own hands, David cried out to God for revenge (his words are recorded in Psalm 7:1–6). God says, "It is mine to avenge; I will repay." (see Deuteronomy 32:35–36).

In My Life

Few things make us angrier than being accused of something we didn't do. As rumors spread about us, or as we suffer consequences we don't deserve, our anger grows until it explodes in revenge. We become determined to make others suffer as much as we have.

The choice between handling things ourselves—getting even—and letting God handle the situation is hard for anyone to make. Thankfully, when Jesus faced a similar situation, He left it in God's hands. Instead of taking revenge on His enemies, He allowed them to curse and mock Him, spread lies about Him, beat Him, and kill Him. Because He did, we are saved from the revenge of sin—eternal death. And because He did, we have the strength in Christ to do the same.

Prayer

Forgive me, Lord, for taking revenge into my own hands. Help me to love those who hurt me as You have loved me. Amen.

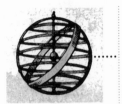

On one occasion an expert in the law stood up to test Jesus. "Teacher," he asked, "what must I do to inherit eternal life?" "What is written in the Law?" He replied. "How do you read it?" He answered: " 'Love the Lord your God with all your heart and with all your soul and with all your strength and with all your mind' and, 'Love your neighbor as yourself.' " "You have answered correctly," Jesus replied. "Do this and you will live." But he wanted to justify himself, so he asked Jesus, "And who is my neighbor?" *Luke 10:25–29*

Something to Think About

As usual you are minding your own business, on your way to the bike rack, headed for home, and not looking for trouble. This afternoon's basketball practice was tough, even for the equipment manager—"More towels!" "Where's my water bottle?" "Can't you ever have my warm-ups were I need them?" And Deion, the most demanding, obnoxious player on the team, had been especially bad.

As you pass the corner of the parking lot, you hear moaning coming from the shrubbery. *Could be an animal caught in the bushes*, you think as you push aside the branches to check. But there on the ground, nose and lip bleeding, clutching his ankle, and crying, lies Deion.

You assess the situation quickly: you don't see the people who did this, but they haven't had time to go very far. You're also pretty sure Deion hasn't seen you yet. You make a list of all the reasons to run for the bike rack and forget you ever saw Deion. You make another list of reasons to help him.

The first list is much longer than the second. It includes... (fill in your own list).

The second list has only one word. Neighbor.

Into the Word

Jesus told a story to answer the lawyer's question, "Who is my neighbor?" A traveler had been robbed, beaten, and left to die. A priest and a Levite passed by, pretending not to see. But a Samaritan stopped, attended to the man's wounds, carried him to an inn, and paid for his care. Even the legalistic inquirer got Jesus' point— the neighbor was the one who showed mercy.

Jesus showed that kind of mercy to you and me, caring so much that He died to save us. Because of His mercy, we can love all of our neighbors. Even Deion.

Prayer

Lord, forgive me for all the times I have not loved my neighbor. Help me to remember Your great love for me—love that took You all the way to the cross. Then make me ready to love and help all who are in need. Amen.

"Be still, and know that I am God; I will be exalted among the nations, I will be exalted in the earth." *Psalm 46:10*

Something to Think About

What do you see when you look at the figure on this page? Look away, then look back again. Do you see it now?

In order to see what's really in this illustration, you must change your focus. You have to focus on the white letters instead of on the black background.

We Christians are often as confused by life as you were at first by this figure. That's because we tend to focus on the background.

We may, for example, focus on possessions—cool clothes, a great CD collection, computers, stereos, a nice car, even friends can become "possessions." All of these vie for our attention, but they're not what life is really about.

In times of trouble, we may fearfully focus on that which terrifies us—conflict at school or in the family, divorce, the future, illness, even death. The more attention we pay to our fears, the more they overwhelm us.

Or we feel so bad about the wrongs we have done to others that we are paralyzed by our guilt. Focusing on our own sin separates us from the forgiveness and acceptance of others and keeps us from God.

Into the Word

The writer of Psalm 46 tells us how to shift our focus. "Be still, and know that I am God," he writes (Psalm 46:10). Moving our focus to God moves it away from the things in our lives that distract and distress us: our desire for possessions, our fears, and our guilt.

We focus on Jesus when we spend time in His Word: in worship, in Bible study, in family or private devotions. We feel His presence in the fellowship and encouragement of our Christian friends.

When we focus on Jesus, our Savior from sin, we receive by faith the righteousness and forgiveness He won for us through His death. When we repent and accept God's forgiveness, we are free to live lives that are pleasing to Him.

Prayer Thought

Ask Jesus to help you focus on Him in all aspects of your life.

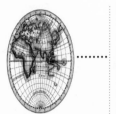

I sought the LORD, and He answered me; He delivered me from all my fears. Those who look to Him are radiant; their faces are never covered with shame. This poor man called, and the LORD heard him; He saved him out of all his troubles. The angel of the LORD encamps around those who fear Him, and He delivers them. *Psalm 34:4–7*

Something to Think About

Sometimes life terrifies me … Violence in my school and my community. My parents constantly fighting, mostly about bills and money. Classes that get harder and harder, and my counselor telling me I'll never get into college. New viruses spreading like ancient plagues. Wars breaking out all over the world.

Then I remember that night in Utah.

It was your made-for-television family vacation. That night we pitched our tent and rolled out our sleeping bags in a desert campground near Moab, Utah, just outside Arches National Monument. The day ended perfectly: a great meal, postcard-perfect sunset, and the sublime feeling of putting tired muscles into a warm sleeping bag.

Half an hour later the wind began to blow. Not breezy little puffs of wind, but the strongest, loudest, most uninterrupted wind I have ever heard. It caught the side of our tent like a giant sail, and only the weight of my father in the corner kept it anchored in place. The assault continued all night—the wind continuously hurling all the sand of southeastern Utah at our family's tent.

Wide awake and terrified, my mind raced through a doomsday list of terrible things that were about to happen to us. But somewhere in the middle of it all, I prayed. Silently, in my heart, I turned the whole situation over to God: the sand storm, my family, everything.

And the most amazing thing happened. The wind didn't stop blowing, at least not until later the next day. Sand continued to pelt us, and the tent strained all night at its poles and stakes. But my terror left me. I felt the presence of God with us in the tent, and I was not afraid.

Remembering that night in Utah, I know what to do when life begins to terrify me. I pray, turning all my fears over to God and remembering Paul's words to the Roman Christians, who also lived in some scary times: "In all these things we are more than conquerors through Him who loved us. For I am convinced that neither death nor life, neither angels nor demons, neither the present nor the future, nor any powers, neither height nor depth, nor anything else in all creation, will be able to separate me from the love of God that is in Christ Jesus our Lord." (Romans 8:37–39). God doesn't always change the situation—at least, not right away—but He never leaves us alone to face the situation. His presence gives us the power to say: I am not afraid.

Prayer

Dear Lord, sometimes life scares me to death. I turn over to You all that frightens me. Assure me that You are with me and have the situation in control, and I will not be afraid. I pray in the name of Your Son, Jesus, my Savior. Amen.

The LORD will fulfill His purpose for me; Your love, O Lord, endures forever—do not abandon the works of Your hands. *Psalm 138:8*

Something to Think About

Dear Mike,

It seems odd to be writing to you instead of sitting down with a pizza and just talking about stuff. I always liked that we could talk about anything. I really miss that.

We'd made so many plans for the future together. How we'd go to computer camp next summer. Which girls we'd ask to go to the homecoming dance. Where we'd go to college and what we'd study and how we'd be roommates. What kind of jobs we'd get after college and where we'd live and when we'd get married.

Who knew Dad's company would downsize, and he'd lose his job! So here we are in California at Grandma's, living in her basement like it's a little apartment. It's pretty crowded and a little tense sometimes, but I guess it'll do until Dad and Mom find new jobs.

But I sure learned a lesson about making plans. At first I was really upset with Dad and Mom—even with God—that they could go and do this after I'd made all those plans. But in my devotions, I was led to read Psalm 138:8. The plans are all still in place, only they're not my plans. They're God's.

I thought about it and realized that it's a good thing they are His plans. I can count on them being good for me. Remember that verse the pastor made us memorize in Confirmation class? "And we know that in all things God works for the good of those who love Him, who have been called according to His purpose" (Romans 8:28).

It looks like there won't be money to go to computer camp unless I get a scholarship. I'm going to fill out the application today. Who knows—it may be in God's plan for me.

Anyway, write soon, okay?

Your friend,

Ryan

In My Life

God has plans for you. They started when you were saved from sin and death through His Son, Jesus. Plans that start out with something that wonderful are bound to be good.

Prayer

Lord, I make plans as if I were the one working things out in my life. Help me remember that You love me, that You are in control, and that you have promised Your plans will be good for me, for Jesus' sake. Amen.

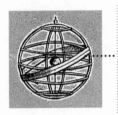

"Therefore I tell you, do not worry about your life, what you will eat or drink; or about your body, what you will wear." *Matthew 6:25a*

In My Life

Worry controls the lives of Christians and non-Christians alike. In His Sermon on the Mount, Jesus gives us seven simple reasons not to worry.

Do you spend so much time worrying about details—what you're going to eat or wear, for example—that you miss what life is about? Remember, God who gave you life can be trusted to handle its details too. "Is not life more important than food, and the body more important than clothes?" (Matthew 6:25).

Do your worries about tomorrow (where you might go to college) interfere with what you need to be doing today (studying for the math test on Tuesday)? Worrying about the future can hamper your present efforts and activities. "Look at the birds of the air; they do not sow or reap or store away in barns, and yet your heavenly Father feeds them. Are you not much more valuable than they?" (Matthew 6:26).

Does it seem to you that worry doesn't get you anywhere? That's because worrying often does more harm than good. "Who of you by worrying can add a single hour to his life?" (Matthew 6:27).

Do you worry because God seems to have forgotten about you? God cares about everything He has made. He especially cares about you, His child whom He has redeemed through Jesus' blood. "See how the lilies of the field grow. They do not labor or spin. Yet I tell you that not even Solomon in all his splendor was dressed like one of these. If that is how God clothes the grass of the field … will He not much more clothe you, O you of little faith?" (Matthew 6:28–30).

Do you worry because you don't understand God's care? Worry shows a lack of faith in God and in His ability to care for you. "For the pagans run after all these things, and your heavenly Father knows that you need them" (Matthew 6:32).

Does worry keep you focused on the wrong goal? God has real plans and real challenges in store for you, and worry keeps you from realizing them. "But seek first His kingdom and His righteousness, and all these things will be given to you as well" (Matthew 6:33).

Has your life become a continuous cycle of worry? Live one day at a time to avoid being consumed by worry. "Therefore do not worry about tomorrow, for tomorrow will worry about itself. Each day has enough trouble of its own" (Matthew 6:34).

Prayer Thought

Make a list of what you worry about most often. Then turn those worries over to God in prayer. "He who did not spare His own Son, but gave Him up for us all—how will He not also, along with Him, graciously give us all things?" (Romans 8:32).

They came to Capernaum. When He was in the house, He asked them, "What were you arguing about on the road?" But they kept quiet because on the way they had argued about who was the greatest. Sitting down, Jesus called the Twelve and said, "If anyone wants to be first, he must be the very last, and the servant of all." *Mark 9:33–35*

Something to Think About

"So, Mark, how did you do on Kettner's history test?"

Mark put his tray down on the cafeteria table, shrugging as he sat down next to Rachel. "Okay, I guess. How did you guys do?"

Henry smiled. "Eighty-nine. Best I've done all year."

"Yeah?" Anne said. "Well I got a 93. How about you, Julie?"

"Not quite as good as all of you—just a 78."

"You guys are no match for me," Jim bragged, setting his tray next to Mark's. "I got another 100, which means I'm still number one in the class."

Into the Word

Jesus' disciples defined success much as Jim did. But Jesus used another standard: "If anyone wants to be first, he must be the very last, and the servant of all" (Mark 9:35). While Jesus wants us to do our best in school and in our jobs, he does not want us to be prideful about our talents and hard work. Instead, we are to use them to further His glory and be servants to others.

Jesus Himself provided an excellent example of this kind of servanthood. He left His throne in heaven and became a lowly human being, taking upon Himself the sins of all people. He died on the cross to save the people He had made, who had turned against Him.

In My Life

What do you plan to do with your life? Do you want to be successful? By whose standard?

Prayer

Lord Jesus, it's easy to get caught up in the world's idea of success. Forgive me for my pride and make me a willing servant of all. Amen.

For I envied the arrogant when I saw the prosperity of the wicked. They have no struggles; their bodies are healthy and strong ... Surely in vain have I kept my heart pure; in vain have I washed my hands in innocence. All day long I have been plagued; I have been punished every morning. *Psalm 73:3–4, 13–14*

Something to Think About

Karen watched the group at the end of the hallway with more than a twinge of envy. Lindsey Tyler was surrounded by her usual swarm of football players all responding to her casual flirtations with obvious enjoyment.

It's just not fair, Karen thought, slamming her books into her locker. *I'm just as pretty and smart as Lindsey and everyone says I'm fun to be with. Does it seem to matter? No. She still gets all the guys.*

Karen turned and watched the group again. Even though Matt had his arm around her, Lindsey reached over and kissed Jeremy on the cheek, smiling at him suggestively.

That's why she's so popular, Karen thought, closing her locker and walking toward chemistry class. *Lord, what's the point of "saving myself" if it means being alone?*

Into the Word

Why do people who act immorally and show no regard for God seem to have such great lives, while those of us who try to live God-pleasing lives suffer in comparison? The psalmist Asaph asked the same question. He struggled with God to find the reason for this apparent unfairness.

But Asaph realized that focusing on his suffering instead of on God had poisoned his thinking. Through faith in God he understood what was really important: "Yet I am always with You; You hold me by my right hand. You guide me with Your counsel, and afterward You will take me into glory" (Psalm 73:23–24). Through faith in our Savior Jesus Christ, we are confident of the promise of eternal life, an eternal reward far better than popularity, or money, or anything else we might desire.

As for the ungodly, who seem to have such a great life now? According to Asaph, we don't need to worry: "Those who are far from You will perish; You destroy all who are unfaithful to You" (Psalm 73:27). And leaving justice in God's hands leaves us strong enough to say, "But as for me, it is good to be near God" (Psalm 73:28a).

Prayer

Lord, sometimes my life doesn't seem fair. Remind me of the riches that are mine in the salvation won for me by Your Son, Jesus. Then keep me faithful to You that I may one day live with You in heaven. Amen.

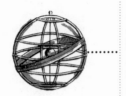

"Whoever wants to become great among you must be your servant, and whoever wants to be first must be your slave—just as the Son of Man did not come to be served, but to serve, and to give His life as a ransom for many."
Matthew 20:26–28

Into the Word

It goes by many names in our world. Social climbing, positioning, one-upmanship, brown-nosing. Whatever you want to call it, a desire for authority appears to have been an obsession among Jesus' disciples. "Who's going to sit next to Jesus in the kingdom of glory?" "Who's going to be most important?"

How often Jesus explained it! Leadership in His kingdom was just the opposite of what they saw around them. "You know that the rulers of the Gentiles lord it over them, and their high officials exercise authority over them. Not so with you," [He told them.] "Instead, whoever wants to become great among you must be your servant" (Matthew 20:25–26).

How often Jesus gave them examples through His service to others! In service to a wedding couple, He turned water to wine and saved the celebration (John 2:1–11). Out of compassion for the multitude, He used seven loaves and a few small fish to feed thousands of hungry people (Matthew 15:32–38). As a servant, He healed the sick, cured the lame, gave the blind sight, and the deaf hearing. His heart went out to the widow of Nain, and He raised her son (Luke 7:11–17), just as He raised Jairus' little girl (Luke 8:49–56).

On the night before He died, as the disciples prepared to eat the Passover meal together, Jesus taught one last lesson in leadership. He wrapped a towel around His waist, poured water in a basin, got down on His hands and knees, and washed their dusty, smelly feet. "I have set you an example," [the Master Teacher explained,] "that you should do as I have done for you" (John 13:15).

In My Life

We recognize Jesus as our Leader, of course. But our Servant?

Our Servant, yes. Not only in all He provides for us, in being the one Friend we can count on to be with us even when everyone else deserts us. Not only by standing with us in all our troubles and making them work out for our good. But most of all, in doing what He came to earth to do— obeying God perfectly (which we could never do), and dying on the cross in our place.

Prayer

Jesus, my suffering Servant, You died on the cross for me. Help me to humbly love and serve others as You did. Amen.

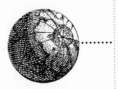

"Woe to you, teachers of the law and Pharisees, you hypocrites! You are like whitewashed tombs, which look beautiful on the outside but on the inside are full of dead men's bones and everything unclean. In the same way, on the outside you appear to people as righteous but on the inside you are full of hypocrisy and wickedness." *Matthew 23:27–28*

Something to Think About

Have you ever visited a movie studio? The tour bus takes you down a street lined with beautiful houses. Some of them look familiar from movies or television programs you have seen. But when you turn the corner and look back, you can't believe what you see. Boards brace up the dreary, unpainted back side of the colorful facades you saw from the street. Behind the front doors of these "houses," instead of cheery living rooms or kitchens, you see piles of junk and stacks of storage boxes.

As Christians, we sometimes try to appear smooth and polished in our faith like the front sides of these houses. We hide our true identity, including our weaknesses and faults, behind a false front.

Into the Word

It was for a similar reason that Jesus was furious with the Pharisees. He criticized them for making a great show of their religion, in everything from what they wore to where they sat at banquets and in the synagogue, to what they wanted other people to call them. He accused them of using the law to shut the door of the kingdom of heaven to other people. He cursed them for observing the finest points of the law (and judging others who didn't) while missing the law's main points: "Love the Lord your God with all your heart and with all your soul and with all you mind.... Love your neighbor as yourself" (Matthew 22:37–39).

The Jews whitewashed their tombs to make them more visible since Jewish law said a person who came into contact with the dead—even stepped on a grave accidentally—was unclean and could not take part in religious ceremonies. So Jesus compared the Pharisees to these whitewashed tombs: "beautiful on the outside, but on the inside full of dead men's bones!"

In My Life

Where is your religion? On the outside, like the Pharisees? Do you worry too much about making sure people see you *act* like a Christian? Are you quick to judge others when their actions don't seem as "holy" as yours? Are you so caught up in church *activities* that you don't have time for church beliefs?

Or is your religion on the inside too? When it is, instead of seeing ourselves as better than everyone else, we recognize our lowly and sinful state—and a need for our Savior. Thankfully, through His death on the cross, Jesus has cleansed the dead bones of sin from our insides, making us white with His righteousness and enabling us to love others with His love.

Prayer Thought

Ask Jesus to give you a clean heart that you may love others.

Nevertheless, more and more men and women believed in the Lord and were added to their number. *Acts 5:14*

Something to Think About

"Next week I'm going to Church A for their youth group. The youth leaders are great—they're young and everyone seems to have so much fun. Last week they did a youth service with skits and jokes. and they always have these great activities planned outside of church. A lot of "cool" people from school go there. That's what a youth group should be!"

"I think I want to join Church B. You should see the food they get for their coffee hour, and it's all free!"

"Church C brings in a guest speaker every month. I finally feel like I'm getting some intellectual stimulation. Church C is the place for me."

"The members at Church D are so friendly. The first time I attended, they all welcomed me, and the next week they even remembered my name!"

"We're planning to join Church E. The sanctuary is so beautiful. It will make a wonderful background for our wedding pictures."

Into the Word

New believers came by droves to the early Christian church in Jerusalem. What attracted them?

Many came because of the miracles they saw the apostles do, miracles that demonstrated God's almighty power. As they listened to the apostles speak, the Holy Spirit brought faith to their hearts. They believed what they heard: Jesus, whom the Jews had crucified, was the Son of God and had risen from the dead. And they were impressed by the love and generosity the Christians showed one another.

In My Life

What attracts you to a church? Youth skits, speakers, coffee hour, and friendly members are fine, but what a church is all about is the message that Jesus came into the world to save sinners by His death on the cross. When you're attracted to a church, look for that message. Without it, you have found only programs, buildings, and a fellowship club. With it, you have found the kingdom of God.

Prayer

So many things distract me from Your kingdom, Lord, even in my church. Keep my mind on the real reason I go to church—to worship You as my Savior. Amen.

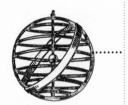

"And when you pray, do not keep on babbling like pagans, for they think they will be heard because of their many words. Do not be like them, for your Father knows what you need before you ask Him."
Matthew 6:7–8

Something to Think About

The gymnast completed her routine and stood waiting for the judges to post their scores. As she waited, she looked nervously around the gymnasium. She smiled slightly as her eyes met her mother's, and she scanned the crowd looking for a reaction from her friends. And all the while her lips kept moving furiously, "Our Father who art in heaven … "

Into the Word

You see it at sporting events, in hospital waiting rooms, during exams at school, at the dinner table, and—perhaps most of all—in church. People reciting a prayer, often over and over, when they're obviously thinking about something else. It must have been common in Jesus' day also, because He instructs the people: "And when you pray, do not keep on babbling like pagans, for they think they will be heard because of their many words" (Matthew 6:7).

Odd, isn't it, from the same Jesus who admonished them to pray continually?

In My Life

But there's a difference between praying and reciting the same words over and over. Incantation—mindless repetition of words—has been practiced since the beginning of time with no results. How could there be? No one is communicating with anyone.

In prayer, however, we are in direct communication with God. We can concentrate on the One to whom we are speaking, remembering that He has asked us to come to Him with our needs as children come to a loving parent. We can be confident that He will listen and answer according to what is best for us. Why? Because He loved us enough to send His son to take the punishment for our sins.

When you're ready to pray, think first about the One to whom you are speaking and what He has done for you. Then communicate—tell Him sincerely what is in your heart, knowing He will listen.

Prayer Thought

To help you focus on God when you pray, thank Him for what He has done for you, especially through His Son, Jesus.

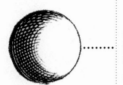

"That is why, for Christ's sake, I delight in weaknesses, in insults, in hardships, in persecutions, in difficulties. For when I am weak, then I am strong." *2 Corinthians 12:10*

Something to Think About

Lord, I'm beginning to wonder if You're listening to me at all. I mean, I've prayed about this a couple times before and haven't felt any change … so I'll ask one more time.

Everything hurts so much. Ever since Mom died, there's so much pain, and I can't stand it anymore. It feels like I'm dying inside too.

Please God—take away this pain. I don't care what happens, what else goes on. I'm too weak and exhausted to care. I just don't want to hurt anymore. Please?

In My Life

Being a Christian does not mean being free from pain. In fact, sometimes being a Christian can be the cause of pain, as many early Christians found out after the first Pentecost. Many were tortured or killed because they preached that Jesus had died and rose again. But pain comes from other sources too, that have nothing to do with being Christian. People we love die or move away, we become sick or injured, we feel alone, unwanted, unneeded.

Sometimes we have the strength to pray as some early Christians did: "Now, Lord, consider their threats and enable Your servants to speak Your word with great boldness" (Acts 4:29). Or rather, don't remove the problem or remove us from the problem, but instead help us to be bold *despite* the problem. But more often than not, we plead, "Take it away!"

Into the Word

In 2 Corinthians, Paul admits this is what he had been praying. But instead of removing the problem, the Lord answered him, "My grace is sufficient for you, for my power is made perfect in weakness" (2 Corinthians 12:9a).

Our pain—human weakness—provides the perfect backdrop for understanding the love and power of God. In our pain, we recognize that we can't survive on our own, we can't save ourselves. We need divine intervention in our lives. And God provides. He gives us the strength, the understanding, the courage, and the love to make it through the pain, whatever its cause.

Once Paul understood this he could say, "Therefore I will boast all the more gladly about my weaknesses, so that Christ's power may rest on me. That is why, for Christ's sake, I delight in weaknesses, in insults, in hardships, in persecutions, in difficulties. For when I am weak, then I am strong" (2 Corinthians 12:9b–10). Can you say this as well?

Prayer Thought

Talk to God about a problem that is bothering you. If it is not God's will that this problem be removed, ask Him for the strength to deal with it according to His will, and the ability to understand His working in your life.

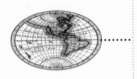

As Jesus was getting into the boat, the man who had been demon-possessed begged to go with Him. Jesus did not let him, but said, "Go home to your family and tell them how much the Lord has done for you, and how He has had mercy on you." So the man went away and began to tell in the Decapolis how much Jesus had done for him. And all the people were amazed. *Mark 5:18–20*

Something to Think About

Suppose you suffered from a rare and fatal disease. You spent what you believed to be the last weeks of your life confined to a hospital room, connected to machines and bottles of medication to ease your pain, a miserable prisoner of your sickness.

Then one day a doctor announced a new treatment for your illness. This doctor happened to be lecturing in your community, and he came to the hospital and administered the new treatment to you. Within minutes your symptoms began to subside, and in a short time you were ready to leave the hospital, free of the disease and its effects on your life.

Reporters and television crews wait for you in the hospital lobby. Your friends want to know what has made the difference in you. Do you think you'll mention the doctor?

Into the Word

The man who had been cured of demon-possession knew what he would say. He asked to follow Jesus, to be one of His disciples and share in His ministry. But Jesus had other plans for him. "Go home and tell your family," Jesus said. So the man returned to the Decapolis, an area of ten Gentile cities primarily east of the Jordan River, to tell everyone what Jesus had done for him and the mercy He had shown him.

In My Life

Do you find it hard to tell others about your faith? Do you think you would need a lot of special training, like the kind a pastor gets at the seminary? Or do you think witnessing should be left to professionals who know how to do it?

Think about the cure for the fatal disease. Who would be the more convincing witness—a professional who had studied the reports of the doctor's research or the person who had been cured?

You are the person who has been cured. As Paul said to the Romans, "all have sinned and fall short of the glory of God" (Romans 3:23). Sin is a horrible, eternal-life-threatening disease because it separates us from God. It would take over every aspect of our lives and eventually destroy us, if it weren't for Jesus. Thankfully, we are not left to die. When we recognize how "sick" we are and ask the Great Physician to heal us, He tells us it's already been done. Jesus' death and resurrection is the ultimate cure, more so because it comes at no cost to us. Paul's letter to the Romans continues, "[all] are justified freely by His grace through the redemption that came by Christ Jesus" (Romans 3:24).

Prayer Thought

Thank God for His healing work in your life. Ask the Holy Spirit to help you tell others about your faith.

"You must be on your guard. You will be handed over to the local councils and flogged in the synagogues. On account of Me you will stand before governors and kings as witnesses to them. And the gospel must first be preached to all nations. Whenever you are arrested and brought to trial, do not worry beforehand about what to say. Just say whatever is given you at the time, for it is not you speaking, but the Holy Spirit." *Mark 13:9–11*

94

Something to Think About

The slumber party had followed the pattern of most slumber parties—lots of party and no slumber. The pizza had been great, as well as the bags of junk food and cartons of soda, and the CDs and videos had provided a noisy background for the long evening of girl "stuff." It was the first time Mandy had been included in the group of popular girls from school, and she couldn't remember when she had had so much fun.

Sometime after midnight, the talk took a more serious turn. Mandy had been reading a magazine, but her ears perked up when she heard the topic change to abortion. "My life and future are too important to be ruined at my age," said Heather. "If I got pregnant, my mom would pay for me to have an abortion."

Several girls nodded in agreement. Then Amy looked at Mandy. "What would you do, Mandy?" she asked.

Mandy froze. She knew what she would do, and wanted to tell the other girls, but she had a strong feeling they'd laugh at her beliefs.

Into the Word

Until that moment Mandy thought persecution of Christians occurred only in other centuries or other places. But according to Jesus, it will confront all Christians. That's OK, Jesus says, because persecution will give you the opportunity to witness to your faith.

In My Life

If you were Mandy, would you worry about what you were going to say? Jesus said, "Do not worry beforehand about what to say. Just say whatever is given you at the time, for it is not you speaking, but the Holy Spirit" (Mark 13:11).

Jesus' words make two things clear. You will not face persecution alone; the Holy Spirit will be with you and will give you the words to say. And if it's the Holy Spirit speaking, your role as His instrument is important.

Your friends may laugh. They may not include you in the next party. They may look down on you for the stand you take. That's persecution; Jesus told you it was coming. But the words the Holy Spirit gives you may make your friends stop and think about what you believe, why you believe it, and if maybe they should believe it as well. Just as the Holy Spirit works in you to have faith in Jesus as your Savior, He can also work in your friends.

Prayer

Lord, make me a bold witness for You in the face of persecution. Send Your Holy Spirit to give me the words to say, and use those words to bring my friends to faith in You. Amen.

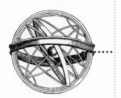

There is no difference, for all have sinned and fall short of the glory of God, and are justified freely by His grace through the redemption that came by Christ Jesus.
Romans 3:23–24

Something to Think About

"John! Hold on for a minute!"

John glanced over his shoulder and groaned inwardly. Pastor Dave was coming from the room where they had just met for youth group. What did he want?

"I just wanted to make sure everything was going okay for you," Pastor Dave said, once he caught up to John.

"Great," John said, putting on his best smile. "Never been better."

Pastor Dave hesitated before answering. "It just seems to me that you've been kind of down. Want to talk about it?"

John glanced down at his hands ... at his wrists, actually. He could still see the angry red lines from where he had cut himself with a piece of glass. He pushed his watch band over them and looked back up at Pastor.

Tell him about his attempted suicide? His attempt to murder himself? Reveal just how horrible he really was? "Nah—I'm just fine. Just a little stressed from school."

Pastor Dave smiled, but John could tell he didn't quite believe him. "Okay," Pastor said finally. "But if you want to talk, just let me know, okay?"

Into the Word

Sometimes we try to assign varying degrees to sin. We'll say, "Oh, it was just a little white lie," or "What I did wasn't nearly as bad as what *he* did." But to God it's all the same. "All have sinned and fall short of the glory of God."

But the good news is also the same. "[All] are justified freely by His grace through the redemption that came by Christ Jesus" (Romans 3:24). And His grace has no time limit. "But the gift of God is eternal life in Christ Jesus our Lord" (Romans 6:23b).

In My Life

John did not want to "come clean" because he did not want to reveal how horrible he thought he was. He didn't think the pastor could understand or forgive. Do you feel the same? Do you wonder if there is anything God can't forgive?

It has been said that the only sin God can't forgive is the one you haven't confessed. Not confessing means willfully holding on to a sin, keeping it out of God's reach, because we don't trust Him to forgive us or because we don't really want to surrender every part of our life to His lordship. In doing this, we reject Jesus and His death for us. We reject the righteousness He offers. We cut ourselves off from His grace.

But remember 1 John 1:9, "If we confess our sins, He is faithful and just and will forgive us our sins and purify us from all unrighteousness."

Prayer

Lord, I confess all of my sins to You. Forgive me for the sake of Your Son, Jesus, and His death in my place. Help me never to reject Your love and forgiveness. Amen.

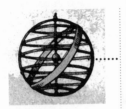

In the sixth month, God sent the angel Gabriel to Nazareth, a town in Galilee, to a virgin pledged to be married to a man named Joseph, a descendant of David. The virgin's name was Mary. The angel went to her and said, "Greetings, you who are highly favored! The Lord is with you." "I am the Lord's servant," Mary answered. "May it be to me as you have said." Then the angel left her.
Luke 1:26–28, 38

Something to Think About

Carrie was the youngest of five children. She knew her parents loved her, but they also equally loved all of her brothers and sisters. At school she was smart, but there were others who were smarter. She played on the basketball team, but wasn't a starter. In short, Carrie knew she was an OK person, just nothing very special.

At church her pastor talked about Jesus dying to save the sins of the world.

"Sure," Carrie thought, "He came and died for everyone. But not specifically for me. I'm not that important."

Into the Word

Long ago God sent the angel Gabriel to Nazareth with a message for an ordinary young girl named Mary. "Greetings," [the angel said.] "You are highly favored. The Lord is with you." Gabriel proceeded to tell Mary that she would give birth to a baby she would name Jesus. This baby would be the Son of God, the promised Messiah.

"I am the Lord's servant," Mary answered with faith-filled acceptance. "May it be done to me as you have said" (Luke 1:38).

In My Life

Through the power of the Holy Spirit, we hear the angel Gabriel speak to us, individually and specifically, the words he directed to Mary: "You are favored. The Lord is with you."

As Gabriel announced the coming of the Savior to Mary, so he announces it to us individually and specifically. God sends His Son, Jesus, the promised Messiah, to live among us—our Immanuel, God with us. He will rule in the hearts of those who love and follow Him, and His kingdom will have no end.

With Mary we respond in faith. "I am the Lord's servant. May it be to me as you have said." And with Mary we praise God joyfully: "My soul glorifies the Lord and my spirit rejoices in God my Savior, for He has been mindful of the humble state of His servant. From now on all generations will call me blessed, for the Mighty One has done great things for me—holy is His name" (Luke 1:46–49).

Prayer

I praise and thank You, Lord, for sending Your Son, Jesus, to be my Savior from sin and death. Amen.

They came to John and said to him, "Rabbi, that Man who was with you on the other side of the Jordan—the One you testified about—well, He is baptizing, and everyone is going to Him." To this John replied, "A man can receive only what is given him from heaven. You yourselves can testify that I said, 'I am not the Christ but am sent ahead of Him.' The friend who attends the bridegroom waits and listens for him, and is full of joy when he hears the bridegroom's voice. That joy is mine, and it is now complete. He must become greater; I must become less." *John 3:26–30*

Into the Word

After the lean days in the wilderness, with only a handful of followers, John the Baptist had finally achieved success. Multitudes came out to the Jordan River to hear him preach and to be baptized by him. Even the Pharisees and Sadducees came, curious to hear what he had to say.

It would have been easy to listen to the adulation of the multitudes, to take their praise to heart. They thought he was Elijah, or a prophet. Some even thought he was the Messiah who had been promised.

But John knew better. He answered them with a quote from Isaiah: "I am the voice of one calling in the desert, 'Make straight the way for the Lord'" (John 1:23). Soon he would say of Jesus, "He must become greater; I must become less" (John 3:30).

In My Life

When things go well in life, we can almost hear the praises of the crowds too. Our ego grows so large that it distorts our perception of reality.

We become so proud of what we have done that we begin to see ourselves as much better than everyone else, maybe even good enough to please God. After all, we've done so well, He's fortunate to have us on His side.

The truth is, nothing we do on our own is pleasing to God. "All our righteous acts are like filthy rags" (Isaiah 64:6). When we are tempted to think otherwise, we need to go back to the message that John preached: "Repent, for the kingdom of heaven is near" (Matthew 3:2).

All our sins, including pride, are forgiven for the sake of Jesus, God's Son who died in our place. But it is only through Christ's sacrifice that we will ever be judged good enough to please God.

Prayer

Lord, I confess that my pride keeps me from seeing myself as the miserable sinner I really am. Forgive me for the sake of Jesus, Your Son. Help me put my ego aside so that I, like John, may point people to Jesus. In His name I pray. Amen.

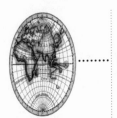

Then He returned to His disciples and found them sleeping. "Could you men not keep watch with Me for one hour?" He asked Peter. "Watch and pray so that you will not fall into temptation. The spirit is willing, but the body is weak." Matthew 26:40–41

Something to Think About

Has your family ever taken a long trip cross-country in the car? As you ride along, you think of something you want to be sure to see—perhaps the first sight of the Rocky Mountains or the bridge over the Hudson River, or maybe the sign for a certain city or national park. But as mile follows mile, the motion of the car and the sound of the engine lull you to sleep, and the next thing you know, your car is parked in front of the motel where you will spend the night. You completely missed what you were waiting to see.

Into the Word

Peter, James, and John really wanted to watch and pray with Jesus. But the day had been long and eventful, and the Garden of Gethsemane was quiet and peaceful. And soon only snoring could be heard in the serene garden.

When Jesus returned to them and found them sleeping, He turned to Peter: "Could you not keep watch with Me for one hour? ... Watch and pray so that you will not fall into temptation"

(Matthew 26:40–41a). Twice more Jesus went off by Himself to pray; twice more the disciples fell asleep. The next thing they knew, Judas and the temple guard had entered the garden to arrest Jesus.

Jesus knew their weakness: "The spirit is willing," He said, "but the body is weak" (Matthew 26:41b). They wanted to pray with Jesus, to share with Him the suffering of this night. But to do that, they had to stay awake.

In My Life

Do you watch out for temptation the way Peter, James, and John watched with Jesus in Gethsemane? If you do, the devil will find you an easy victim. With your brain in neutral, your mind unaware of what is happening, you will readily fall into behavior you know is against God's will for your life. Instead, wake up! Be alert and aware, constantly on the lookout for the devil and his tricks. "Be self-controlled and alert," [a more mature, Spirit-guided Peter wrote later.] "Your enemy the devil prowls around like a roaring lion looking for someone to devour. Resist him, standing firm in the faith" (1 Peter 5:8–9a).

And don't forget to ask for help. "Watch and pray," said Jesus. Ask for His help in resisting temptation and His forgiveness for your sins.

Prayer

Help me, Lord Jesus, to resist temptation. You know my spirit is willing, but my body is weak. Strengthen me through Your Word and Sacraments so that I don't give in when I am tempted. Amen.

He asked them, "Do you believe that I am able to do this?"

"Yes, Lord," they replied.

Then He touched their eyes and said, "According to your faith will it be done to you"; and their sight was restored. *Matthew 9:28b–30a*

Something to Think About

"See, so as long as you have faith …"

Lisa tuned the rest of the pastor's words out. Have faith? How was she supposed to have faith in something—Someone—she couldn't see? How did she know He was really there?

All her life she had been told about God, about how He created the world and sent His Son to save the world, and so on and so on. She knew all the stories by heart; they'd been drilled into her enough. But now that she was older, she was really beginning to wonder. What if it was all a lie?

Pastor Michaels finished his sermon and the organist started playing the offering hymn. Lisa had the hymnal open on her lap, but she couldn't bring herself to start singing.

Did she really not believe in God?

Lord, help me! She whispered in her mind, then stopped. Did she even believe He *could* help?

Into the Word

Two blind men heard of Jesus' healing powers. They learned where He had been teaching and healing others and followed after Him.

"Have mercy on us, Son of David!" they called, and continued to follow Him.

Jesus asked them, "Do you believe that I am able to do this?"

In My Life

Spiritually speaking, we're often nothing more than blind men and women sitting by the side of the road. We can't *see* God. We don't know what He looks like, or where He is, or even if He's really there. We're lost in darkness and can't see His Light.

And in darkness, it's pretty easy to believe that there really is nothing—or no One—there.

The two men were asking Jesus to heal their physical blindness. Today, we ask Him to heal our spiritual blindness. He healed the blind men, and by virtue of His death and resurrection, He can heal us. But He asks one question first:

"Do you believe I can do this?"

Prayer

Lord, I do believe, but help me overcome those times of unbelief. Amen.

John said to the crowds coming out to be baptized by him, "... Produce fruit in keeping with repentance. And do not begin to say to yourselves, 'We have Abraham as our father.' For I tell you that out of these stones God can raise up children for Abraham." *Luke 3:7–8*

Something to Think About

Ryan had to admit he had enjoyed the pastor's visit, up until now. What he hated most about being in the Juvenile Detention Center was boredom, and any visitor relieved that, even one wearing a clerical collar. Besides, Ryan enjoyed hearing the pastor talk about the outside world.

But now the pastor's questions began to make Ryan a little uncomfortable. All this stuff about God and confessing sins against Him and getting His forgiveness and living differently because of Him ...

"I know I've got a problem with the courts, Pastor. They've got me for stealing the car, and they'll probably give me extra time for the drug charges and breaking and entering. I realize I'll have to pay my time for what I did as far as the state is concerned. But I guess I never worried about God. After all, my parents are your best church members. They're at church every Sunday and a couple nights in between. I figured I was all right with God because of them."

Into the Word

John the Baptist ran into the same attitude when he called the Jews to repent and change their lives. Proud of their heritage as descendants of Abraham, they relied on *his* righteousness and *his* relationship with God for their salvation. But John had news for them: "Out of these stones God can raise up children for Abraham" (Luke 3:8).

Instead of relying on some kind of earthly connection, John urged his listeners to work on their relationship with God. Turn from cheating and lying, he said, show mercy and deal fairly with each other. And most important, John pointed them to Jesus, the Messiah, who would soon be among them and would baptize with the Holy Spirit and with fire.

Then one day, Jesus Himself came to John to be baptized. As John stood in the Jordan, he saw the heavens open and the Spirit of God descend like a dove upon Jesus. "This is My Son, whom I love," [said a voice from heaven,] "with Him I am well pleased" (Matthew 3:17).

In My Life

Righteousness and salvation do not come from our earthly fathers and mothers; they can only come from our heavenly Father. He sent His Son to die for us, to win that righteousness for us on the cross. But it is in our Baptism where God says, "This is My child, whom I love," that we are clothed in His righteousness forever.

Prayer

Heavenly Father, I have sinned against You and against other people. My parents' beliefs do not keep You from seeing the wrong I have done. But Jesus has died for me, so when You look at me, see only the righteousness of Your Son. In His name I pray. Amen.

When the Sabbath came, He began to teach in the synagogue, and many who heard Him were amazed. "Where did this man get these things?" they asked. "What's this wisdom that has been given Him, that He even does miracles! Isn't this the carpenter? Isn't this Mary's son and the brother of James, Joseph, Judas and Simon? Aren't His sisters here with us?" And they took offense at Him. *Mark 6:2–3*

Something to Think About

Derek was barely able to get through the acceptance letter from Harvard without yelling in excitement. He had been chosen to go to one of the best schools in the country—and given an incredibly nice scholarship as well.

He stuffed the letter back in the envelope and wondered who he could tell about it. He could just hear his mom: "That's nice, dear. You can ride out to Boston with your sister since she's already at MIT."

His father: "Well, since I went there, how could you not get in?"

Mr. Watkins, his English teacher: "Oh, all of you Taylors have always done so well. Both of your sisters and your brother were straight-A students. Good to see you were keeping up!"

His girlfriend: "Good job, Derek. But then, didn't we all say you'd get in?"

Derek sighed, and stuck the letter in his back pocket. Like anyone would ever actually acknowledge that I can do great things, he thought. I can't wait to get out of here and go where no one knows me.

Into the Word

The people of Nazareth thought they knew Jesus. He was the carpenter's son, after all. They saw His brothers and sisters every day. They were amazed at His wisdom and miracles, of course, but saw no reason to believe He was any different from anyone else in Nazareth. Their preconceived notions kept them from recognizing the Son of God.

And Jesus was amazed at their lack of faith.

In My Life

Don't let your preconceived notions about Jesus keep you from really getting to know Him. Read His Word, the Bible. Learn more about Him in Bible studies and in church. Learn to see Him for the amazing and loving Savior He is. That way, you can truly understand what it meant for Him to die on the cross and rise again—for you.

Prayer Thought

Ask God to help you get past your preconceived ideas about Jesus and to help you understand better who He is and how He works in your life.

Then Jesus asked them, "Which is lawful on the Sabbath: to do good or to do evil, to save life or to kill?" But they remained silent.

He looked around at them in anger and, deeply distressed at their stubborn hearts, said to the man, "Stretch out your hand." He stretched it out, and his hand was completely restored.
Mark 3:4–5

Into the Word

Think of some adjectives you would use to describe Jesus. On the basis of the stories we read in the gospels, your list might include such words as "kind," "loving," "friendly," "caring," and "good." Would you have chosen the word "angry"?

But the gospels' writers tell us of several instances when Jesus was angry. Mark records one occasion when Jesus went to the synagogue on the Sabbath and met a man with a shriveled hand. The Pharisees were also there, waiting to see how Jesus would handle the situation.

Jesus felt compassion for the man and wanted to heal him, but both He and the Pharisees knew that healing the man would break the Jewish laws about working on the Sabbath. Jesus wanted to use the situation to prove He was Lord of the Sabbath; the Pharisees wanted to use the situation as fuel for their plot to have Jesus killed.

Jesus knew the Pharisees' thoughts, so He asked, "Which is lawful on the Sabbath: to do good or to do evil, to save life or to kill?" (Mark 3:4) And both He and the Pharisees knew the implications of the question: By planning to kill Him, the Pharisees were the ones who would be guilty of breaking the law. Jesus grew angry, but instead of doing anything to the Pharisees, He healed the man's hand.

In My Life

The Pharisees' hypocrisy and concern for the appearance of keeping the details of the law instead of caring for another human being made Jesus angry. Perfect, holy Jesus. Isn't anger a sin?

Anger itself isn't wrong. It depends what happens next. Jesus didn't lash out at the Pharisees because He was angry; He didn't do anything to hurt or harm them at all. Instead, He healed someone.

How do you handle anger?

Anger can easily grow to hatred, and hatred to hurting the person with whom you're angry. Anger can lead to resentment or revenge. Anger can destroy the person who doesn't know how to use it for good.

But anger can also be a powerful force to accomplish good, the impetus that moves you to correct a situation in which someone is being treated unfairly, to help someone who has been hurt or ridiculed, to share Christ's love where it has not been shared before. When *you* get angry, what happens next?

Prayer

Lord, forgive me for the times I let my anger turn to hatred and hurting. Help me channel my anger into correcting wrongs and helping those around me who have been the victims of injustice. In Jesus' name I pray. Amen.

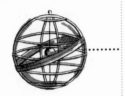

Some of those present were saying indignantly to one another, "Why this waste of perfume? It could have been sold for more than a year's wages and the money given to the poor." And they rebuked her harshly. "Leave her alone," said Jesus. "Why are you bothering her? She has done a beautiful thing to Me. The poor you will always have with you, and you can help them any time you want. But you will not always have Me." *Mark 14:4–7*

Something to Think About

"All right, everyone," Steve said, trying to keep the youth group's attention. "The last thing we have to talk about is what to do with the $5,000 that Mrs. Crawford gave us. Any ideas?"

"Big party?" Tony suggested, and several others laughed.

"I say we use it to make food boxes for the homeless," Amy said.

"We do that with all the other money we raise," Tina said. "How about we use it to plan some kind of youth service? Either out at the park, or maybe do a big musical or something."

The other kids just stared at her. "Why would we do that?" Tony asked, and his friends laughed again.

Tina shrugged. "I don't know, just to do something special to praise God."

Into the Word

Jesus' disciples struggled with a similar dilemma. Mary had anointed Jesus with an alabaster jar of perfume worth more than a year's wages. The extravagance of her gift left the practical disciples dumbfounded. "It could have been sold—and the money given to the poor," they argued.

But, according to Jesus, Mary's unselfish act of worship was right. She had given much—perhaps all she had—to worship Him.

In My Life

What is your worship like? Practical? Enough to get by? Just going through the motions? Or is it extravagant and unselfish like Mary's?

Instead of sitting with the hymnal open in your lap, try singing along, making the effort to understand what the words are saying. If your mind tends to wander, follow along in the Bible when the Scripture lessons are read. Try to apply the points of the pastor's message to your own life.

And don't forget another important part of worship—the offering. Is your gift what's left over after your other expenses, or is it generous, lavish—like the gift of salvation that Jesus has given you?

Prayer

Help me, Lord, to worship You extravagantly, with all my being, because of all You have done for me. Amen.

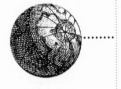

As Jesus started on His way, a man ran up to Him and fell on his knees before Him. "Good teacher," he asked, "what must I do to inherit eternal life?" "Why do you call me good?" Jesus answered. "No one is good—except God alone. You know the commandments: 'Do not murder, do not commit adultery, do not steal, do not give false testimony, do not defraud, honor your father and mother.' " "Teacher," he declared, "all these I have kept since I was a boy." Jesus looked at him and loved him. "One thing you lack," He said. "Go, sell everything you have and give to the poor, and you will have treasure in heaven. Then come, follow Me." At this the man's face fell. He went away sad, because he had great wealth.
Mark 10:17–22

Something to Think About

Have you ever played the kind of video game that resembles a maze? As you progress through the various screens, whether you are escaping from aliens or searching for a treasure, you find your path blocked by a formidable obstacle. Attempts to go around the obstacle place you directly in the path of a monster or your archenemy. The only thing you can do—the only way to win the game—is to completely remove whatever is blocking your way.

Into the Word

In Mark 10, we read about a man who found he had a pretty big obstacle in his way—his love of money and possessions. While he thought he had done everything he could to inherit eternal life, Jesus made him see he had not done the one and only thing that would guarantee him a place in heaven: give up his trust in himself (his money and possessions) and rely totally on God.

In My Life

Our lives are also full of obstacles. Think about it for a minute. What stands between you and eternal life? Possessions? Friends? The desire to be popular? Obsession with sports or fitness, leisure activities, even school? Whatever you allow to become more important in your life than God separates you from Him, and keeps you from eternal life with Him in heaven.

Alone, you cannot go around or remove that obstacle. But once you recognize that it blocks your path and ask God to remove it for you, He does, through the death and resurrection of His Son, Jesus.

Prayer

Forgive me, Lord, for letting other things become more important in my life than You. For Jesus' sake, remove the obstacles that separate me from You and eternal life. Amen.

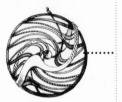

Then Peter came to Jesus and asked, "Lord, how many times shall I forgive my brother when he sins against me? Up to seven times?" Jesus answered, "I tell you, not seven times, but seventy-seven times." *Matthew 18:21–22*

Something to Think About

Laura stared at the wrinkled front end of her father's car, trying hard not to cry. She could still hear the sickening screech of brakes and still feel the impact of the car against the telephone pole.

"Laura! Laura, are you okay?"

Laura jumped at her father's voice. She hadn't realized he'd gotten there yet.

"Oh Dad—Dad, I'm so sorry!" She was afraid to look at him. This was her third accident this year. Even though this was the first time it was her fault, she knew he'd be furious.

But instead of yelling, he came up and hugged her tightly. "It's all right, honey. I'm just so glad you're OK." He pulled back to look at her. "You are OK, right?"

"I'm fine. But, Dad—I totaled your car."

"Shh," he said softly, pulling her back against his chest. "Just forget about that for now."

Into the Word

Jesus came to teach the world about His Father's forgiveness, a kind of forgiveness much different from that taught by the world. For instance, Peter had learned from the Rabbis that he should forgive people who had offended him three times. Peter knew Jesus probably taught something different, so he asked, "Lord, how many times should I forgive my brother when he sins against me? Up to seven times?" (Matthew 18:21).

Jesus told him, "Not seven times, but seventy-seven times" (Matthew 18:22). In other words, every single time, without keeping count. Then Jesus told him a parable about a servant who had been forgiven an enormous debt by his master, but refused to forgive a small debt owed him by another servant. See Matthew 18:23–35.

In My Life

When we read Jesus' story, we see all too clearly that we have behaved like the unforgiving servant. We refuse to forgive others, even though God in His mercy has forgiven us an enormous debt—our rebellion against Him and His control over our lives, our selfish pursuit of our own interests and pleasure, our loveless behavior toward the people God has given us to love. He sent His Son, Jesus, to take upon Himself the punishment for all our sin, to die in our place. Because of Jesus, God declares us righteous—totally debt free!

When someone sins against us (a small offense compared to our long list of sins against God), we remember Jesus. Instead of keeping track of the times we're supposed to forgive our neighbor, or refusing to forgive altogether, we ask Him to give us an attitude of forgiveness like His.

Prayer

Heavenly Father, forgive my sins for the sake of Your Son, Jesus, and give me a forgiving heart, so that I might forgive others as I have been forgiven. Amen.

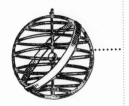

"Again, it will be like a man going on a journey, who called his servants and entrusted his property to them. To one he gave five talents of money, to another two talents, and to another one talent, each according to his ability. Then he went on his journey. The man who had received the five talents went at once and put his money to work and gained five more. So also, the one with the two talents gained two more. But the man who had received the one talent went off, dug a hole in the ground and hid his master's money." *Matthew 25:14–18*

Something to Think About

Ken knew he was good at football. He'd been a varsity starter since his sophomore year of high school, and even made the all-state team his senior year. But he worked hard to make himself even better, especially once he was in college. In the long run, it paid off. Athletic scholarships covered more than half his tuition for all four years of college—and he helped lead his team to a number of division championships.

Sarah had always liked to sing. A friend of her family gave her voice lessons while she was growing up, helping her learn and practice the techniques that would make her a better singer. She dreamed of one day singing professionally, but for now she was happy singing in the school choir and especially the church choir. Mrs. Murphy always commented on how much more beautiful the services sounded when she sang.

Peter's English teachers always told him he could write well; he always got A's on his papers. He did like writing and thought that maybe in college he'd study it—maybe become a journalist one day. But when Mrs. Bolton asked him if he'd help out with the school newspaper, he said no. I *better not waste my time with that*, he thought. There are better things to do.

In My Life

God has given each of us a variety of resources. These include talents and abilities, time, health, and material possessions. While it may seem to us that some people have received more resources than others, we have all been blessed.

Make a list of the resources God has given you. Do you use them all? Or do you sometimes hide them?

If your friends were to make lists of their resources from God too, would their lists be longer or shorter than yours? What resources would be on your list and not that of your best friends? What resources would they have that you have not been given?

Now look at your list again. God gave us His best resource of all—His Son, Jesus, to die for our sins. How can *you* use each resource on your list to serve God and other people?

Prayer

Lord Jesus, forgive me for selfishly burying the resources you have loaned me. Help me to invest them wisely, generously, and joyfully in the building of Your kingdom. Amen.

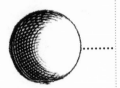

The older brother became angry and refused to go in. So his father went out and pleaded with him. But he answered his father, "Look! All these years I've been slaving for you and never disobeyed your orders. Yet you never gave me even a young goat so I could celebrate with my friends. But when this son of yours who has squandered your property comes home, you kill the fatted calf for him!" *Luke 15:28–30*

Something to Think About

Kevin threw his towel onto the bench, barely resisting the urge to kick something. He couldn't even believe Coach!

Kevin had been practicing hard all week in preparation for tonight's playoff game. He'd even put in some extra time after the rest of the team left, so he'd be ready when Coach put him in the starting lineup.

Except Coach put Frank in instead. Frank, who had been out for two weeks on probation. Frank, an all-star player who had been caught drinking in the school parking lot. Frank, who'd come back "begging" the coach's forgiveness.

Couldn't Coach tell it was an act? *I'm the one who deserves to play, not Frank,* Kevin thought angrily. *So why am I on the bench?*

Into the Word

Kevin, like the older brother of the prodigal son, had a reason to feel bitter. After all, both felt they had been treated unfairly, and then expected to forgive and forget. It simply wasn't fair.

But think about the rest of the parable Jesus told. The younger brother had demanded his inheritance money ahead of time, then wasted it partying with his friends. When his money ran out, so did his friends, leaving him alone and destitute. He meant to return home as a servant, but instead his father welcomed him with a hug and a celebration, forgiving all he had done. "Fair" would have slammed the door; the joyful father forgave.

The bitter brother focused on himself and the unfair way in which he had been treated. Because he couldn't forgive, he never shared the father's joy in his brother's return. And his bitterness kept him from knowing the joy of his father's love because of all the years they had spent working together.

In My Life

Are you bitter because you feel you have been treated unfairly? Does your bitterness keep you from forgiving the person who wronged you and experiencing a good relationship with him or her again?

True, life isn't always fair. Don't let it make you bitter; instead, remember this: God hasn't been fair with you either. Instead of punishing you as you deserve for your sins against Him, He punished His Son, Jesus. He forgives you and welcomes you back to His family, for Jesus' sake. And He enables you, through the Holy Spirit, to share His love and forgiveness with others.

Prayer

Thank You, Lord, for forgiving me instead of treating me as I deserve. Give me a loving heart to forgive others as you have forgiven me. Amen.

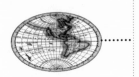

However, if you do not obey the LORD your God and do not carefully follow all His commands and decrees I am giving you today, all these curses will come upon you and overtake you: ... The sights you see will drive you mad. *Deuteronomy 28:15, 34*

Something to Think About

It's enough to drive you mad.

Two boys, aged 9 and 10, hold a 5-year-old by his ankles from a window high in a Chicago Housing Authority apartment. Finally growing bored with the child's screams, they drop him to his death.

A teenager walks into his school in Jonesboro, Arkansas, and guns down several of his schoolmates who have gathered for prayer.

A van loaded with 5,000 pounds of explosives parked at the Alfred P. Murrah Federal Building in Oklahoma City explodes, killing 168 people and injuring more than 500 others, including children in a day care center housed in the building.

In My Life

Do you ever feel that you will go mad if you hear about one more bombing, murder, rape, or other example of human cruelty? If God is in control, why does all this happen?

It's not the way God planned it. The evil we hear about on the news is the result of sin, of our failure to acknowledge and serve God above all else and to love our neighbors as ourselves. Our anger explodes into murder, our self-centeredness into hatred and violence.

We could point our fingers at murderers, bombers, and rapists and feel righteous about ourselves. But Jesus' words condemn us all: "I tell you that anyone who is angry with his brother will be subject to judgment ... anyone who looks at a woman lustfully has already committed adultery with her" (Matthew 5:22, 28). And we are all guilty as charged.

But God had the ultimate solution for sin. He sent His Son into this evil world to live as a man. Then He died on the cross as the sacrifice for the sin of all people, rising again to show His power over sin and death.

We only need to turn back to the news to see that the killing and violence haven't stopped. But remember: the outcome has already been determined. Jesus has defeated sin and death. He will return to judge the world. And He will take everyone who believes in Him, the sinners made holy through His blood, to heaven to live and reign with Him forever.

Prayer

Almighty God, look on the madness of our world and have mercy on us. Forgive me for making myself a part of it more times than I can count. Help me share Your love with a world that needs it desperately, for Jesus' sake. Amen.

"You have heard that it was said,
'Eye for eye, and tooth for tooth.'
But I tell you, Do not resist an evil
person. If someone strikes you on
the right cheek, turn to him the
other also." *Matthew 5:38–39*

Something to Think About

Tim stepped into the batter's box and looked out at the pitcher. Alex Nelson might not be the fastest pitcher at Clearbrook High, but he certainly had the reputation for playing the dirtiest. From the dugout, Tim had observed that many of his pitches to Lamont High's batters in the first two innings had been inside—way inside. Because Tim was a pitcher too, he knew Alex was using intimidation as his main tactic.

Alex's first pitch pushed Tim back. *He's aiming directly for my arm,* thought Tim, *and the umpire acts like he doesn't see what's going on.* Two more fast balls, both way inside, and then Alex threw one right down the middle. Tim's grounder barely made it to the shortstop, who threw him out at first.

In the third inning, Alex faced Mike Watson, Lamont's best hitter. Mike had doubled in the first, scoring two runs. Tim watched as Alex shook off the sign from the catcher, glanced at his third baseman, and threw directly at Mike's head. Mike went down in a heap.

The players in Lamont's dugout turned to Tim. "Alex comes up to bat again in the next inning. You know what to do," they said.

As Alex approached the plate, he looked out at the pitcher's mound. But Tim knew his calm, confident face told Alex nothing. Alex struck out on three of Tim's finest pitches. Alex hit another batter in the fifth, but again Tim threw only his best stuff.

In the locker room after the game, Tim's teammates looked for a scapegoat. "We wouldn't have lost if you had thrown at Alex the way he threw at us. You should have taught him a lesson. You said you knew what to do."

"I did know what to do," said Tim, "and I did teach him a lesson. Doing what is right is always the best way to get even."

Into the Word

The writer of Proverbs wrote, "If your enemy is hungry, give him food to eat; if he is thirsty, give him water to drink. In doing this, you will heap burning coals on his head, and the LORD will reward you" (Proverbs 25:21–22). It's the kind of revenge Jesus used, and it's the kind of revenge in which His children, who are forgiven by His blood, can have complete confidence.

Prayer Thought

Ask Jesus to forgive you for wanting to get even, and to help you not return violence for violence.

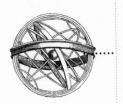

On that day a great persecution broke out against the church at Jerusalem, and all except the apostles were scattered throughout Judea and Samaria.... Those who had been scattered preached the word wherever they went. *Acts 8:1,4*

Something to Think About

Kim hated the thought of moving. She couldn't help but wonder how this could be God's plan for her life. After all, in Chicago, besides the house she had lived in all her life and people and places she was familiar with, she had the greatest youth group—friends she had known since kindergarten and with whom she had been able to share her faith and grow spiritually. She had even been able to attend a Christian high school with other students who believed as she did.

But her dad had been transferred. She would have to find new friends and a new youth group in Oregon. There was no Christian high school in the town where they would live, so she would have to attend a public school for the first time. What if the students there made fun of her faith? What could God possibly have in mind?

Into the Word

The early Christian church faced a similar problem. Persecution scattered the first Christians throughout Judea and Samaria, and they missed the fellowship they had known in Jerusalem. Gone were the sermons of the apostles about the salvation they had witnessed in Jesus' life, death, and resurrection. Gone were the breaking of bread and prayers together. Gone too was the communal society in which everyone shared their goods and took care of those in need. The early Christians must have wondered what God had in mind.

But as reported in Acts, "Those who had been scattered preached the word wherever they went" (Acts 8:4). What God had in mind was exactly what Jesus had told them when He ascended to heaven: "You will be my witnesses in Jerusalem, and in all Judea and Samaria, and to the ends of the earth" (Acts 1:8b). Persecution forced them to leave the life they had enjoyed in Jerusalem and proceed with God's plan—to witness to the world.

In My Life

Have you been complaining about a problem in your life that doesn't seem to fit God's plan? How could God be using this very problem to prepare you for the work He has for you to do?

We never know what God has in store for us, or how or where God will use us to further His kingdom. His plan for us may include something as drastic as moving across the country or to another part of the world—or may be as simple as who we sit next to in classes or in the cafeteria. But no matter what happens to us, we find comfort in these words in Jeremiah, " 'For I know the plans I have for you,' declares the LORD, 'plans to prosper you and not to harm you, plans to give you hope and a future' " (29:11).

Prayer

Forgive me, Lord, for putting myself first when I look at Your plans for me. Help me see that You are in control of my life and will use me for Your glory. In Jesus' name. Amen.